The SEVENTIES

Good Times, Bad Taste

Alison Pressley

Picture Acknowledgements
The publisher would like to thank the following for supplying photographs and illustrations for this book:

Front cover:
Dorling Kindersley: Lasser digital watch; Polaroid SX-70 camera
Advertising Archives: 3, 4 top, 5 below, 14 below, 15, 16 below right, 17 both, 19 below, 24 top left, 50 below, 69 top, 80, 81 both, 84
Camera Press: 9 below
Coloursport: 89 top
Corbis: 9 top © Bettman /CORBIS, 12 below © Wally McNamee/CORBIS, 16 top © Neal Preston/CORBIS, 21 © Barnabas Bosshart/CORBIS, 40 top © Hulton-Deutsch Collection/CORBIS, 41 below © Bettman/CORBIS
Ronald Grant Archive: 42 top
Hulton Archive: 29 below, 83, 90 both, 91, 99
PA Photos: 65, 67, 89 below
Pictorial Press: 16 below left, 39, 40 below, 56
Popperfoto: 54, 55, 58 below, 62, 98, 111
Rex Features: 8, 10, 30 right, 33 top, 35
Vin Mag Archive: 49 top right, below right, 64

The author and publishers have made every reasonable effort to contact all copyright holders. Any errors that may have occurred are inadvertent and will be corrected in subsequent editions if notification is sent to the publisher.

The publisher would also like to thank Ron Callow, Nigel Fountain, Jack Harris and Judith Palmer as well as the author and the author's friends for the loan of personal photographs and memorabilia, and apologizes if the name of any individual contributor has been inadvertently omitted.

First published in Great Britain in 2002 by
Michael O'Mara Books Limited
9 Lion Yard
Tremadoc Road
London SW4 7NQ

A CIP catalogue record for this book is available from the British Library

ISBN 1-85479-690-9

1 3 5 7 9 10 8 6 4 2

Designed and typeset by Design 23
Edited by Gabrielle Mander

Printed and bound in Singapore by Tien Wah Press

Dedication To Laura

Acknowledgements

The following people were kind enough either to allow me to interview them on videotape, or to phone or email me snippets of memories. I am indebted to them all, especially as I had never met the majority. They were, to a person, insightful, interesting, and candid about their deeds during the decade that taste forgot. **Maggie Alderson, Helen Allen, Keith Austin, Anne Bush, Pauline Cornell,** **Quentin Craven, Jane Curry, Louise Egerton, Jeremy Evans, Barry Goodman, Karen Hanks, Peter Hanks, Julie Hart, Peter Hart, Roy Jackson, Mick Jarvis, Frances McKenna, Brian Parker, Rosemary Parker, Fiona Scaife, Anne Shillito, Diana Simmonds, Jean Walker, Steve Walker**

I would also like to acknowledge those kind friends who pointed me in the direction of many of the above—and in some instances provided the meeting place, not to mention essential refreshments guaranteed to lubricate the interviewing process: **Carol Dix, Peter and Janet Garland, Vicki and Neal Gordon, Ray and Pat Kirby, Caroline Lurie**

I am as always indebted to my sister **Valerie Grove** for her tireless pursuit of luminaries or budding luminaries of the decade, bullying and cajoling them into providing the stories scattered through the text. I am also extremely grateful to those same people – **Tina Brown, Carmen Callil, Jonathan Coe, John Diamond, Stephen Fry, Valerie Grove, Joyce Hopkirk, Frieda Hughes, Caitlin Moran, Blake Morrison, John Walsh, Francis Wheen, Victoria Wood** – for their fascinating experiences and anecdotes.

Finally, I must acknowledge my gratitude to Lesley and Michael O'Mara for their faith in and backing of the series, and to **Gabrielle Mander,** editor and publisher *sans pareil*.

Putting this book together was a gas. I hope you'll have as much fun reading it.

Introduction

This book is the third in a series chronicling some of the decades of the twentieth century, beginning with *The Best of Times: Growing Up in Britain in the 1950s* and continuing with *Changing Times: Being Young in Britain in the 1960s*. Like the others, the idea behind *The Seventies: Good Times, Bad Taste* is to build up a snapshot of the decade by presenting the experiences, opinions and anecdotes of a selection of mostly unknown people. There is no intention of serious social or political analysis; these are simply recollections that typify how and why young people felt and behaved as they did in that tumultuous decade—and the more bells that are rung in readers, the better. That's the goal.

But this is the first book in the series not to mirror my own experiences and feelings. I was still young in the seventies—in my twenties, at least; but I was not a teenager. And I did not spend the whole decade in Britain. At the end of 1973 I left England in a Kombi van, intending to spend two years hippie-tripping around the world; I have yet to return to live. Some of those who travelled with me have yet to return at all.

My experience of the second half of the decade in Britain, therefore, consisted of intermittent visits back when the coffers allowed. And what I saw disturbed me greatly. Each time

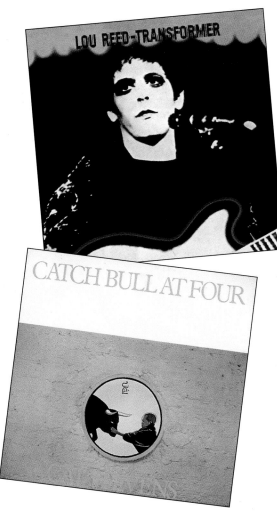

I talked to people born between 1955 and 1960, give or take a year or two. People whose formative years were the seventies, that strange decade that started off slavishly following the sixties, gave birth to punk, and ended up voting Margaret Thatcher into power.

I wasn't disappointed. It was, I discovered, a much more complex decade than my heyday, the sixties. Darker, deeper, edgier. Listening to the stories I was fascinated, amused, appalled, aghast, delighted. I hope you will be too.

I returned the cities seemed dirtier and more neglected, the social problems more acute, the people more radical and politicised. Not to say polarised. Yet the energy and ideas and enthusiasms of my friends and acquaintances, and of the writers I read and the broadcasters I watched and listened to, were undiminished. This has always been, and I hope always will be, a nation to inspire and lead. A month in Britain is worth a year elsewhere.

So it was with great curiosity that I embarked on the interviews that resulted in this book. For once, I was not talking to my peers.

Contents

The Spirit

'A very strange decade'

The Style

The look: from hippie to punk

The Sights and Sounds

Music, dancing and the media

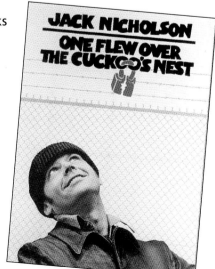

The Lifestyle

Daily life in the seventies

The Wider World

A decade of decline, disillusionment – and defiance

The Spirit

'A very strange decade'

When you're young, a decade is a long time. It can mean the difference between being at school and being a parent. People remembering their youth in the seventies fall neatly into two separate groups: those for whom the exciting changes of adolescence and early adulthood transcended the upheavals of the decade, and those whose memories are blighted forever by the twin evils of being overshadowed by the sixties and living through some of the biggest challenges Britain had faced since the Second World War. Which side are you on?

Good times ...

It's a total transition, that period between being a child and being an adult. It's like a caterpillar to a butterfly. Everything happens in your teenage years, doesn't it? And for me it was the start and finish: getting an education, meeting people, meeting my wife, having a child. Total change. It was a brilliant time. I loved studying, and I got away from Wolverhampton.

The seventies are important to me because that was *my* time. I had Led Zeppelin, and Free. I had a great time.

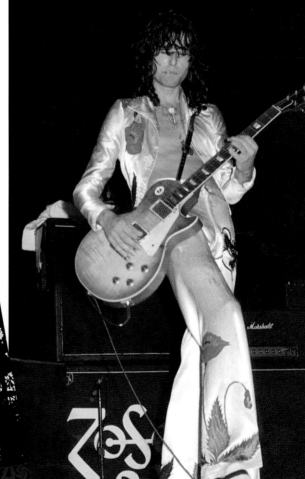

STEPHEN FRY

Author of several novels, a memoir (*Moab Was My Washpot*) and performs as an actor and entertainer, as guest or host on chat shows. In *Who's Who*, lists his hobbies as smoking, drinking, swearing and pressing wild flowers.

The seventies, ah, the seventies. 'A low, dishonest decade' like Auden's thirties, or 'that discredited decade' as Tebbit once weirdly called the sixties?

I find it hard to separate the decade from my own teens, which would have been what they were in any age and any decade. If there is a single image it is that of the frayed edge of flared loon/jean bottoms

shredded by bicycle chain and mud. The newsreel of three-day weeks, petrol shortages and strikes is something laid on memory by the current spate of seventies retrospective, so my own experience has been taken over by Channel 4 researchers who were barely divided nuclei in their mothers' wombs at the time. Public school progressive rock, now called Heavy Metal, was more important than the glam-rock singles that have now taken on a kind of retro-chic.

It was innocent if by innocent one means I knew nothing of drugs, and my only access to thoughts of sex was from libraries and bibliographies. Today they have late night on Channel 4 and the internet. It didn't feel innocent at the time, however; it felt lurky, sly and furtive.

Everything in my life had been leading to the point that started in 1976/77, when my entire universe expanded. It was like, life is a university, life is a party. It was exciting stuff.

I had a lot of freedom in the seventies that I wouldn't have had had the sixties not happened. I was able to live away from home, I was able to have a car, at quite a young age.

It was a pretty good time. Everyone went about enjoying themselves, pubbing it, clubbing it. Experimenting with drugs.

The great thing about the seventies was the women's movement. The lives of western women changed totally in this decade.

For me, the seventies means feminism, women's lib, and the realization that I didn't have to end up like my mother's generation, which had worried me for a while. You didn't have to be married the minute you left school, and have housekeeping money from your husband. I had a very good time in the seventies.

I went from a hardworking kid to a huge success story. It was a good feeling, a good decade.

In the seventies, for the first time in my life, I told my parents what I believed in, instead of just going along with whatever they wanted.

The middle seventies, when I was sixteen, seventeen, were great – first date, first boyfriend, all that sort of thing.

I led quite a sheltered life. But I had a good seventies. I look back on that time with great affection.

There was a lot of idealism at the time, of which I felt myself to be a part.

I'd quite happily go back and do it all again – and soak it up more thoroughly the second time around. It was wonderful.

It's a decade I look back on as one of great fun and of optimism.

I really enjoyed the seventies. I packed a lot into them, and travelled a lot, and got out of England just before everything began to crumble.

... bad times

The seventies? Politically, culturally, in every way, the decade that's best forgotten.

All of the decade was just bad news after bad news. It was all about windswept council estates and concrete. A lot of it was so bleak. It was vile.

The seventies was a decade in mourning for the previous decade. The whole of the seventies was about being sad that the sixties were over and that we'd missed it. The Sex Pistols' refrain 'No Future' was how I felt about my life.

It was a dark decade, politically, economically, and it was also the beginning of our awareness of environmental problems.

None of us expected to get jobs when we left school. So many people felt as though they were on the human scrapheap, especially those who came from a deprived background.

I wasn't very happy during the seventies, but I did live. I didn't think being happy was where it was at, anyway. It was being on the edge, really living. I worked hard at that.

It was a decade of complete upheaval. You had the strikes, you had the three-day week, politics were all over the place; you had punk halfway through, which threw everything up in the air. Everything got slightly wilder.

You had to almost get the seventies out of the way. Everybody kept talking about how fantastic the sixties were all the time, and we didn't seem to have a coherent style, it was all fragmented.

I can remember clearly thinking that it was a decade I'd rather not have grown up in.

It was quite frightening, really. At school, you'd be told that most of you would leave and not find a job. You wondered for your future. There were so many strikes going on, and you heard your parents talk about us being the lame duck of Europe. You worried about these things.

There was a lot of peeling away of the fantasy of the sixties, about what the future could bring. Realism really hit hard. The seventies were a lot more volatile than the sixties.

You came out of the sixties, where there was this huge optimism, things were going to change. By the time you got to the seventies, everything was crap. The economy was crap, everyone seemed to be on strike every other day. It was a miserable time. It bred a lot of social unrest, a lot of gratuitous violence. *A Clockwork Orange* summed up the feeling of a lot of people in 1971. I knew people who could have acted in that film quite easily.

It was a decade of violence and problems. It certainly wasn't a time of peace and love. There was definitely a harder edge to everything.

There was an element of the old Chinese curse, 'May you live in interesting times'. The cracks were opening up. It was a very strange decade.

The Style

The look: from hippie to punk

The sixties flowed into the seventies in a very unbordered way, style-wise. A large proportion of Britain's youth seized on the hippie look of the late sixties and took it to extremes. Clothes got more and more outlandish, going from flowing, floaty garments for both sexes, to crazy flares, outrageous platform shoes, skin-tight tops. Then, for some, along came punk and turned everything upside-down.

Out-sixties-ing the sixties 1: clothes

In the early seventies my friends and I got more and more heavily into the hippie scene that began in the late sixties. We girls wore fringed shawls, long skirts, embroidered cheesecloth blouses. We stopped wearing make-up or bras, and wore flat sandals on our feet. The guys wore velvet trousers or jeans with embroidered inserts in the legs to make flares, grandpa shirts or artist's smocks, à la P.J. Proby, and grew their hair and moustaches longer and longer.

I still remember my first Laura Ashley dress. It was long, empire line, with long sleeves with frills around the cuffs. It was made out of musty dark blue velvet cord with a dark red flower pattern, and I thought it was just gorgeous. It made me look pregnant, which was a useful thing on the tube.

I remember driving across country for three hours to go to Laura Ashley's first shop, a tiny little thing in mid-Wales, because my mother had read about it in the *Sunday Times*, or maybe *Nova*.

I really got into the old peasant look, Laura Ashley prints and corduroy, lots of corduroy.

I was crazy about crochet. I crocheted myself a lacy black shawl, then a black top in granny squares with flared sleeves. I wore them together and must have looked like a walking spider web.

I remember buying some brocade fabric at a market and making caftans for myself and my boyfriend, with elaborate frogging fastenings. We wore them with flared jeans; I'd sewn flowered inserts into the outside seams.

I wore a headband to a party in 1970 and felt very hip and cool – until a friend came along and pulled the headband down over my eyes. He did that every time I pushed it back up on to my forehead, and in the end I gave up.

Do you remember tie-dyeing? And batik? Everyone had to have a tie-dyed T-shirt, then later a batik skirt or shirt.

There was a craze for long, hooded cloaks. A girl in our shared house and I got identical black cloaks, and we'd walk around feeling – and no doubt looking – like the French lieutenant's woman.

I considered myself to be a hippie. I enjoyed the hippie ethos, the hippie music and all the famous things that went with it. My older brother had always had music around by people like The Doors, Hendrix, Dylan and so on; I was very influenced by that, so I gravitated towards people who had that same sort of a philosophy, if you can call it that. You were either a hippie or you were straight.

I still have a big RAF greatcoat I got when I was sixteen in 1970; I still wear it.

I got my mother to take a pair of flared jeans and put that extra triangle in to make them wider. She must have thought I was a complete nut. You couldn't see my feet, and I've got big feet.

I started buying antique clothes. I'd go to Portobello Road every Saturday morning. I got my first fur coat there; wearing fur then was perfectly acceptable. You'd just wear a dress and a fur coat, and you could stand at bus stops without fear.

We used to embroider everything, and tie-dye everything. I embroidered a 'Ban the Bomb' sign on the knee of a pair of jeans, and this old boy came up to me in a pub one night and said, 'You don't know what you're talking about; if we'd banned the bomb we wouldn't have had peace in Europe,' and really it was just a fashion statement, nothing political at all.

I bought beautiful, long satin and silk nighties, and I'd wear them as dresses. When I met my future mother-in-law for the first time, I stayed at their place overnight and about eleven in the morning she said, 'We're having lunch soon, dear, aren't you going to get dressed?' I was outraged.

Being heavy and freaky and only ever wearing jeans and cords and shaggy shirts was a big thing, and if you wore desert boots you were really in. It was all about how hippie-ish you could look.

In those days there were two kinds of young people: people who still lived in the sixties, with long hair and beards, lots of Maharishi stuff, incense and all that, and heavy rock music. And there were people like me, who were into bright colours and sparkles and spangles.

Those Afghan coats

I remember having a very smelly Afghan coat that we had to throw out, because it was still alive. I got it from Ashford market. It smelt *so* much …

My brother went to Afghanistan, as you could in those days, and came back with the smelliest, *smelliest* kind of yak-skin coat. It had to live in a special cupboard at home.

I was into the hippie look: embroidered denim and maxi skirts. I had a big floppy denim hat with a flower in the middle of the brim, denim platform shoes with flowers on, and some brushed denim flares with red, white and blue stars embroidered down the insert.

I had a black satin jacket with big rounded lapels. I wore it with loons – and now I know why they were called loons. We looked like a bunch of nutcases.

You had two-tone loons, and they were always frayed around the edges because you stood on the bottom of them. Then when you ran for a bus they wrapped themselves around your legs and you fell over.

I bought my boyfriend a beautiful white Afghan coat, ankle-length, one Christmas. And a few days later we were all dancing at the pub – because we all used to dance at pubs, all the time – and of course we put all our coats in a pile on the floor, and that was the end of it. Never seen again.

I had a lovely dark blue Afghan coat with embroidery all around it. It used to make me feel like a real hippie, even though it was one of the more refined types, not smelly at all. Not really authentic.

The decade that taste forgot

The seventies were constantly revived in the nineties, after we'd reviled them as the decade that style forgot during the eighties. But what people actually wore in the seventies was hideous, because there wasn't a source of good cheap clothes around.

Clothes in the seventies were awful. Just dreadful.

You were either really boring or you were weird; there wasn't much middle ground.

At the beginning of the seventies I had this outfit I was so proud of, I thought I was the bee's knees – although at the same time I remember, very clearly, this flash of thinking, My God, I'm glad this is fashionable, because if it wasn't I would look like a complete idiot. Because it was grotesque. I was a tall girl, but I wore these bright yellow boots, with platforms on them about two or three inches, on top of a four-inch heel. They looked like bright yellow surgical boots. With them, I wore a pair of fake patchwork jeans with little bits of velvet sewn into them here and there. They were desperately uncomfortable because the seams dug into you, they were so tight. When you took them off your skin looked like a grid map. I wore them rolled to the knee so that all the glory of the yellow boots showed. Then on top of that I wore a yellow skinny-rib polo-neck

jumper and a wool safari jacket, big blue and yellow checks, a cross between Noddy and Rupert Bear. That was the seminal seventies outfit for me.

I remember wearing incredibly wide flares. I looked just like a Gumby.

I was thirteen or fourteen at the beginning of the seventies, and my mother had the most awful job getting me into flares. She'd use expressions like, It's the thing, and I had no idea where she got that kind of language from. However, once she got me into flares, it was virtually impossible to get me out of them.

The seventies? They mean the Bay City Rollers; trousers that didn't cover your socks; guys who wore cargo-type trousers with pockets on the sides that stopped way above their boots; enormous knots on their ties, collars outside their jackets. So unsexy.

I had a very long Dr Who-type scarf to go with my trendy midi-coat and platform boots. One day I was getting off the bus and it got caught in the doors when they closed. I nearly choked to death.

Tight, tight trousers. I remember taking in the inner seams of trousers on my sewing machine so I could hardly walk. I'd wear them with high heels. That whole Roxy Music, glam look. Shiny little vinyl handbags shaped like a brick, with little handles.

I got into glam rock, I used to wear satiny hot-pants and I always wore black nail polish – I had immaculate nail polish on for about fifteen years. And you always put glitter over whatever make-up you were wearing.

I thought Noddy Holder was great. I started wearing these really loud checked trousers with great big platform boots, clumping around the place.

I remember wearing a 'uniform' of Levis, brogues, Ben Sherman shirts, Crombie jackets and short hair.

It was the skinhead era. I don't think any of us realized any of the politics behind it. It was all very naïve; lads with shaved heads and girls with ponytails and Sta-press trousers on, and checked shirts.

It was the period of Slade, Bay City Rollers, and we were teenagers so we were very fashion conscious. We'd wear baggy pants, Slade hats, electric green parallels – outrageous clothing. I remember my father saying to me, When you grow up you're really going to regret having worn that sort of stuff. We said, No, no, this is the fashion, Dad; you're square. You're past it,

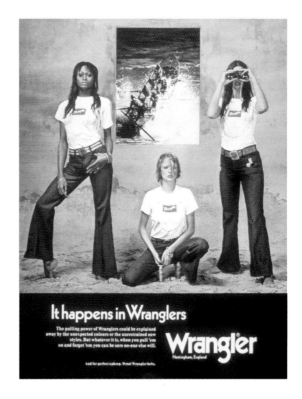

It happens in Wranglers

The pulling power of Wranglers could be explained away by the unexpected colours or the unrestrained new styles. But whatever it is, when you pull 'em on and forget 'em you can be sure no-one else will.

Wrangler
Nottingham, England

And for perfect upkeep, Wear Wrangler belts.

You can make a fantastic break in THREE PIECE SETS at Man at C&A. Sweater, tunic and flare-bottomed trousers. Full-stretch freedom from knitted Orlon/Antron. Colour combinations black/purple, black/orange, camel/white. Sizes 36 to 40. At only £10.19.0 a set, you might fancy pocketing the lot.

Man at C&A

and this is the future. Well, it didn't even last the decade – it didn't even last twelve months before you'd think, God, did I wear that?

I used to have a 'Budgie' jacket. It was light-blue and dark-blue patchwork, short. And I had a 'baby' jacket, which was furry, bright red. I wore it with bright red furry hotpants.

I had a pair of 'skirt pants'. They were wide as they come, full-length, black. I wore them with a yellow cowl-necked jumper. I remember going to the speedway at Bellevue wearing this outfit, thinking I was the bee's knees.

When the Bay City Rollers were in, tartan half-mast trousers were a real fashion item, we all wore them.

It was all about excess. You had to have the widest bell-bottoms, the biggest collar, the biggest hair.

The way I dressed in the seventies gave my father endless bouts of mirth. We used to go on holiday to a caravan in Devon, and I'd go swimming wearing a Slade hat, which was basically a cloth cap, like somebody who had whippets would wear in the north-east, but it was made out of bright Stewart tartan. It was the talking point of the beach.

There was this awful layered look; we were so cluttered up. We had maxi-skirts and midi-skirts with these smocks over the top, blouses with huge billowing sleeves, large collars, silly little beanie hats, platform shoes.

I was very much into the male fashions of the time, things like Crombie coats, Jaytex shirts, two-tone trousers, black Oxford shoes, Rambler jean jackets. And pretty short hair. That was my era. I suppose we were follow-ons from the skinheads. We were known as suede-heads.

Brushed-cotton flares in four or five different colours. Tight knitted jumpers. My mum knitted me a Fair Isle sweater; they were all the rage. Very fitted shirts, body shirts.

the Cream

Gina Fratini
Floating, frilly, flowery cotton makes the prettiest pini with a full sleeved cotton voile blouse. Sizes 10, 12, 14.   £40

Miss Selfridge
Duke Street and Knightsbridge

My girlfriend made me a coat, a long, brown barathea coat, almost to the floor, quite heavy. Split from the waist. Last time I saw one of those was in *Withnail and I*.

The fashions were great. It was brilliant to be able to wear things like baggy trousers, loons, platform shoes, tank tops, big blousy sleeves, minis and maxis. Chelsea Girl in Leeds was the shop to go to. You went on Saturday with your hard-earned cash and you bought cheap tops and T-shirts.

I had a pair of white twenty-three-inch-bottom flares and platform shoes and I thought I was it.

All my friends wore tights, and these huge clompy six-inch platform shoes. I wanted tights and cork wedges so badly, and my mother wouldn't let me.

You had to wear Levi jeans, they were the best. Wranglers were second-class, then it was Lee.

Miss Selfridge was the epicentre of my world in Watford. We went every Saturday. It had all these wonderful clothes. I was fortunate in that I had a groovy mum, so I was able to get the platforms and the flares. I had platform cork clogs, and I thought they were wonderful.

At one invitation-only disco, I was just the business. I wore black wooden and leather clogs. I had a pair of lovely flared shrink-to-fit Levis. I remember lying on the ground and my younger sister pulling on the top of the zip with a coat hanger to get them to do up. The fat was spewing out the top, it was just terrible. I had this piece of leather round my neck, very very important, it was a thong but you had a special knot just at the right place. Lots of black eyeliner – still quite sixties eye make-up – and a peachy-coloured lipstick. I had long hair with a centre parting, and I did tiny little plaits at either side then pulled them back, like loops, to tie at the back. Then

bright red Kickers with yellow laces – and stuff like that. Feminism had its own fantasy gear, of course: a mixture of Romanian gypsy and Welsh coalminer, with a bit of early Diane Keaton for intellectual credibility.

My party outfit by 1979 was red suede basketball boots with silver stars, a black jumpsuit with lots of zippers which was habitually open to the navel or thereabouts, and a lot of shaggy hair. Some of this hair wasn't on my head, but on my legs and under my arms.

All that hair

Hair was really bad in the seventies. My older brother had girlfriends with long, terribly straight, very close to the head hair. Hair was always greasy, too, whether it was yours or anyone else's.

I had an Afro perm in the late seventies that my hairdresser talked me into and my father was incredibly angry about. I had to buy a special comb to keep it curly, with four prongs on the end. I looked like Kevin Keegan.

I had this shirt that was just the bee's knees, because it was made of newsprint fabric.

We all walked around in trousers that had to have a width at the hem of at least eighteen inches, we'd measure them. Then all of a sudden, overnight, real cool people were wearing ankle stranglers, and you wondered how the hell they got them on. Bell-bottoms, flares, bags, parallels, whatever you wanted to call them, went out overnight.

By the late seventies, *Annie Hall* had happened, and so had feminism's ideas of comfortable clothing and shoes. Clothing that didn't pander to male fantasy. So I started going around in baggy pants, baggy shirts, workboots –

FRIEDA HUGHES
Born in 1960. Poet, painter and writer of fiction, she has had several exhibitions and won awards for books. Married to the Hungarian-born painter, Laszlo Lukacs.

In 1973, aged thirteen, I got my first pair of platform shoes, with a half-inch-thick sole and a one-and-a-half-inch heel. I longed to be old enough and slim enough to wear a mini-skirt before they went out of fashion. I gave my brother my half of the train set in exchange for his half of a second hand record player. I spent all my pocket money on my first single, 'Roll Over Beethoven', to shock my father. It did.

In 1975, I sewed extra panels into the sides of my jeans to make them really flared. Stopped throwing my poetry away. Discovered blue eyeshadow and Mary Quant perfume and *Jackie* comics. And motorbikes. I wanted a Laverda Jota – very very badly. I was fascinated by the Sex Pistols, but hated the noise they made. In 1976 my first poem was published, under a pseudonym.

In 1977 I was cut from the wreckage of a Mini in which I was a passenger by two fireman with a circular saw. I had to learn to walk again. The hospital couldn't find me a wheelchair – or an ambulance to take me home. Some things haven't changed.

I remember getting a pair of second-hand bottle-green velvet trousers, and a mustard-coloured crocheted bikini.

In 1978, I told the school careers adviser that I wanted to be a painter and a poet. I left home at eighteen, to become a waitress at 26p an hour, until I could afford it. Discovered hire purchase. Found that I'd missed the mini-skirt moment – but sixteen years later, I decided to wear them anyway.

My older brother used to pin his long hair up when he went to school. And one day a teacher said to my mother, Don't think I don't know that John pins his hair up, because the pins fall out all over the floor.

The Farah Fawcett flick! I wanted that hair, the big flick, and I had a styling wand that had a shot of steam when you pressed a button on the end. I used to basically burn my hair every time I went out, you could smell the scorched hair. But I loved it, I had all my flicks and my curls.

In the late seventies I had a wash-and-wear perm, I had to use an Afro comb on it.

Hair was very important. It was very long, and it had to be permanently flicked. My friend Sue's hair was thicker than mine and it held the curl, it was always perfectly flicked. A bit of Yorkshire rain on mine and it was back to the straggle. You had to use lots of hair spray.

I got into the air cadets big-style in the seventies, from the age of thirteen to eighteen. I was a cross between somebody out of the air force, and a hippie. I was constantly battling between having my hair short enough to be acceptable on parade, and long enough to look like a hippie. But I could wear this shabby old air force greatcoat to cadets, and also out socializing. I looked like Neil out of *The Young Ones*.

I came home from university once and shaved off my moustache, and my girlfriend wouldn't look at me.

When I was sixteen I had hair down past my shoulders. I didn't have any problems with it at school or as an apprentice, all the lads looked like that then.

Friends at college had that feathered look, where you hacked away at your hair with a razor, like Rod Stewart.

I had a Purdey cut. Remember those?

I was getting a bit too old, at twenty in 1977, to walk around in a bin-bag with a Mohican. But I did realize it was probably time to cut my hair, that as a male with long hair I was in a minority. It was a great relief, actually, much more comfortable.

I had a Jane Fonda *Klute* haircut, all feathered around your face – that took a great deal of effort, keeping it feathered around your face.

In the sixties I'd almost been a skinhead. By the time the skinheads really emerged and became

fashionable, in the early seventies, with reggae music and everything, we'd all been through that, and I had hair down to my shoulders.

At school, you couldn't have short hair (because of the skinheads) and you couldn't have long hair (because of the hippies). It was truly bizarre behaviour by adults. Slade and the National Front were very popular in Wolverhampton, Slade started as a group playing to nightclubs of skinheads. So I had moderate-length hair because that's all you were allowed, then as soon as I got to college I grew it because everybody else did.

We were clean, I suppose, but you bathed on a Sunday night and you washed your hair on a Sunday night, and went for days and days without washing your hair in between. Showers didn't exist. And for girls certainly, the mythology was that you didn't wash your hair while you were having a period. Wherever did that come from?

I've had a very ambivalent attitude to body hair ever since the seventies. I tend to shave the pits when I remember to, almost always in summer, but I do hate hairy legs.

I gaily abandoned shaving my legs when feminism decreed that such things were beneath us. (I always shaved my armpits because if I didn't it was really hard not to smell in hot weather or when wearing jumpers.) Then one day I was sitting next to a male friend on a beach, and he looked at my hairy legs and said, You know, that looks bloody awful. I was angry with him, but I still shaved my legs later that day. And I've shaved them ever since.

Finishing touches

Getting ready to go out took ages. Ages, to get it all perfect. Lots of lip-gloss. Miss Selfridge lip-gloss, on a wand. Then we had roller-ball lip-glosses, flavoured strawberry and mint. They were so thick and gooey! Lots of glitter, gold everywhere.

I had Hai Karate aftershave; I think my mum bought it for me one Christmas. That, and Brut. You'd splash it on before going out. Brut was *big*.

I wore lots of bright blue eye-shadow, always blue. Then there was a girl in *Coronation Stree*t in the late seventies who wore very glamorous eye make-up, lots of browns, so I started wearing brown.

My friend Debbie had a white Formica dressing table and these tiny little

Fabergé for the love of life.

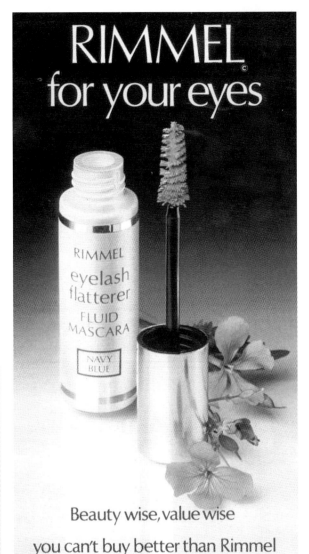
bottles of Vanda perfume, which was the cheap version of Avon. Terrible stuff. They were square bottles with square lids. Oh God, I remember it so vividly! It was really cheap and nasty, and I wanted it so badly because my friend had it.

I could tell you every product in the Number 17 and Rimmel make-up ranges in 1976, and how much they cost. The lip-gloss was like a stick of wax, and they did two nail varnishes in pearlescent. One was pinky-green, and one was turquoisey-silver. There was a lipstick called Marron Glacé.

We wore these enormous sanitary towels that were made out of wads of cotton wool, and they had loops at the ends and you wore an elasticated belt that your mother passed down to you. You bought these from 'the woollen shop' because that's where ladies shopped, and they were wrapped up in paper to be discreet, but nothing else came in that size or shape. We had these awful burners in the toilets at school, incinerators; the smell of burning cotton wool came down the corridors. You had to plan your whole life around it.

The lads who didn't wash in our school would be taken out of the lesson and given a bar of carbolic soap and sent to the showers.

I remember thinking I was so glamorous because at one point I smoked those black Sobranie cigarettes with gold tips, and you could get cocktail ones in different colours. I didn't really smoke but I went through a phase of thinking that was cool.

I had a lovely round three-colour eye shadow palette, with shades of light, medium and dark grey, from Boots Number 17. And I just thought I'd arrived.

Nobody did blusher or foundation or anything in those days, because that was what your mother wore.

I had this really dark blue eye shadow, midnight blue, from Biba. I'd only wear it occasionally because it was so dramatic.

When I was twelve or thirteen and starting to buy clothes – not with my own money yet, my mother was still in control – women wore things like nylons and suspender belts, went to bed in curlers, wore bright red lipstick, and I thought, Oh my God, I don't want to do any of that. And then tights were invented, and along came hotpants, and you could wear tights with hotpants. So I've never worn nylons and suspenders, and I've never been to bed with my hair in rollers.

Is there anything you can't wear?

Plastic jacket Kate Summergood at Queen Street Studios, sandals and bag Mrs. Howie; reassurance by Panty Pads. No loops, no belts, smaller and snugger, an adhesive.

At seventeen I had a French boyfriend who had a Gitane permanently on his lip. I thought he was the sexiest thing, because he'd smoke it on the edge of his mouth, with his eyes half closed.

I was one of the first people to have what in those days were called umbromatic lenses, and what are now called photochromic. You had your normal glasses, and they'd go dark in the sun. They were the last word in *Starsky and Hutch* chic. You'd walk into a room and your glasses would still be dark from the outside. You didn't think about looking like a Mafioso. And they were always slightly tinted – another great seventies invention.

You always had to have a decent pair of boots, a new pair for each winter. Long boots. We paid a fortune for them.

I hero-worshipped my friend in those days, because she was tiny and beautiful and I was very large and lumbering. I had huge feet, size 7 when I was eleven. Debbie had these tiny little brown shoes with large plastic heels, lace-ups, and they came from this shop called Hilton's that my mother would never let us go into because they didn't do shoes in real leather. We had to go to Clarks.

I remember going off to a shoe shop and making the most awful face because I didn't

have a pair of wet-look shoes. So my mother bought them for me, and they cost £5, which was a phenomenal amount then.

Cowboy boots were fabulous for lots of reasons. First of all, they made you taller. Secondly, you could have cleats on the end. Incredibly useful for walking around feeling more important than your stature might otherwise indicate. The best things to wear with cowboy boots were Fiorucci jeans, which had a zip on the back pocket.

I remember wearing clogs at one stage. Do you remember men wearing clogs? I think the fashion only lasted a couple of months.

I had some beautiful pairs of shoes, lots of different suedes, wedges, platforms. Most with much higher heels than I'd wear now, and I'd walk miles in them from bus stops and stations.

I used to love platforms, because I'm tiny. I even had platform pumps, trainers.

Punk style

Punk had its own style. We had to make all our own clothes, or customize them, or we had to find them in jumble sales. I wore black jeans, and old men's jackets that were much too big. Sometimes I'd wear a plastic carrier bag as a T-shirt. One of my looks was a man's shirt worn as a dress, with very high heels and spiky hair and black make-up and lots of studded things. We wore lots of fishnet, used lots of those things called D-rings, ex-army stuff. We were always dyeing things black. It was very creative.

I had a T-shirt from the shop Seditionaries, run by Malcolm McLaren and Vivienne Westwood. It had a print on it by a gay artist from the fifties, a picture of two cowboys wearing cowboy hats, and they've got no trousers on, they've got

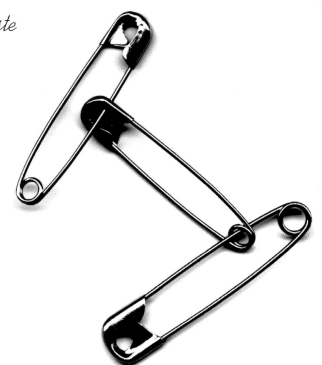

these enormous penises and they're talking to each other. Me and my friend Paula both had them, and we wore them one day in Camden High Street. We went for breakfast at a greasy spoon, and our food had just been put in front of us when a police car screeched to a halt outside and we were arrested and dragged off and charged with obscenity. We had to go to Lavender Hill Magistrates' Court, and the policeman said to us, Oh you're just middle-class girls playing at this, we'll see you in that courtroom with your hair all combed. I just thought, Fuck you. So we went to that court in full punk regalia. But the terrible thing is, I know we got off because we were middle-class. I said, I don't see any difference between this penis and the penis on Michelangelo's David, and the magistrate agreed with me. He let us off with a conditional discharge.

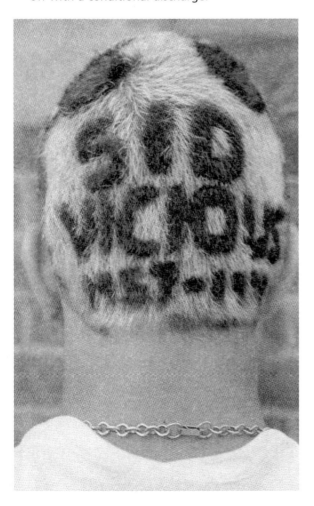

I had a pair of bondage trousers from Vivienne Westwood's shop Seditionaries. They had a fly zip that went right up around your tail bone, zips down the back of each leg, a bondage strap and a clip-on towelling 'nappy', perfect for sitting in gutters.

I had spiky hair but I didn't have a Mohican, because it was my last year of school. I was a bit of a respectable punk.

If you looked at me and my group of friends at the time, you wouldn't have thought we were associated with the music we were associated with, punk. I've never been radical in my appearance.

I didn't have a pierced nose but I had a chain that went from my pierced ear to my nose, where I clipped it on, and I got thrown out of every pub in Stafford, no one would serve me.

I was aware of the punk look, but I was never outrageous in my fashions. Ilkley is a very tranquil part of the world. I've only ever pierced my ears!

The Sights and Sounds

Music, dancing and the media

Just like clothes, early seventies music was an extension of the hippie era of the late sixties, dominated by the twin streams of the California sound and glam rock, with a steady background of soul. Again, the arrival of punk turned everything upside-down. The seventies also saw the advent of Woodstock-inspired weekend-long outdoor rock concerts – except that, here, they had to contend with British weather. Inside, disco reigned supreme, along with pogoing and the beginnings of the mosh pit. On the box, nothing got near the influence of *Monty Python*.

Out-sixties-ing the sixties 2: music

The first teenage crush I had was on Roger Daltrey of The Who. My brother bought *Tommy* and I immediately stole it from him and became obsessed with Roger Daltrey, and had pictures of him all over my bedroom walls. Then I became obsessed with Joni Mitchell, and with Bob Dylan.

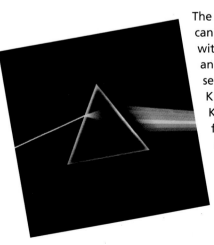

The music was great. I can remember going with my brother Mike and all his friends to see Pink Floyd at Knebworth Festival. Knebworth was a fabulous, beautiful country estate. They had some huge thing in the air, I think it was a blimp. I can remember returning with Mike, and us both agreeing that, while we didn't believe in God, the nearest thing to God on this earth was definitely Pink Floyd. They understood us.

My rich boyfriend and I used to go out on Saturdays and he would buy maybe four LPs. He introduced me to American music: Joe Walsh, Supertramp, the Eagles. He had a new Renault 5 with quadraphonic sound. In the evenings we'd light a joint and get on to these flyovers and listen to the fabulous music.

I still have a collection of LPs from the seventies – or, as my son recently called them, 'those big CDs you have'. I used to work at weekends and after school on Fridays in a pie-and-mash shop at Bethnal Green. And I'd come out of there and walk up the road, straight into the record shop, and I'd buy a couple of albums, every week. It was what we did.

I remember 'All Right Now' coming out in 1971, which I still think is one of the greatest pieces of music ever written. Very simple, but great.

The music of the early seventies was wonderful. Starting with Neil Young's *After the Goldrush*, James Taylor's *Sweet Baby James*, Carole King's *Tapestry*, Cat Stevens's *Teaser and the Firecat* and Carly Simon's first album. It just got better and better: the Moody Blues, Rod Stewart, Lindisfarne, The Doors, Pink Floyd. I remember one guy telling me that hearing David Bowie's *The Rise and Fall of Ziggy Stardust and the Spiders from Mars* was 'just like coming home'. Crosby, Stills, Nash and Young. Buffalo Springfield. The Eagles. Fabulous music. But it all began to go a bit haywire halfway through the decade.

I liked underground music: *The Old Grey Whistle Test* and John Peel on Radio One. Groundhogs, Pink Floyd, Emerson, Lake and Palmer, Jethro Tull.

I listened a lot to Donovan, T. Rex, that sort of gentle sound that was a hangover from the sixties, really. And folksy stuff, Fairport Convention.

Rod Stewart's 'Mandolin Wind' was one of the best songs of the seventies.

I still feel that the seventies left a legacy of very good music, even though some of the music of the time was really pretentious and pompous and silly. People like Emerson, Lake and Palmer, who perhaps more than anybody were pompous and silly. But groups like Genesis and Pink Floyd and King Crimson produced some superb music that still stands entirely on two feet. It wasn't all bad taste.

David Cassidy or Donny Osmond?

In the early seventies you had to make a decision: am I going to go slightly oddballish and follow T. Rex, and be known as a hippie and despised by a large sector of the community, or am I going to go for the clean-cut Donny Osmond/David Cassidy look? I was a T. Rex fan; I couldn't take the Osmonds' teeth seriously at all.

I wasn't into Slade or T. Rex, I was the nice girl on the block, so it was, Are you into Donny Osmond or David Cassidy? I was always a David Cassidy fan. On a Saturday morning, when the magazine *Jackie* plopped through the door, I would hope there'd be a poster of David Cassidy in there so I could put it on my wall.

I liked David Cassidy and Donny Osmond and David Essex. A friend of ours in class liked the Bay City Rollers and we looked down on her, we thought that was too awful.

I was mad about David Cassidy – he was my favourite. I had a poster of him on my wall. David Essex I loved too, in *Godspell* and that whole scene. A gorgeous Cockney boy with beautiful blue eyes.

Glam rock, funky soul

I was very much into soul music. When I was about thirteen, fourteen, Monday nights at the Lyceum in the Strand were a big thing. Monday was soul night, and my friend and I would be two of the few white faces there, because it was a big black night. Lots of funk. When we started to go there we'd just stand and watch these black guys dance, and thought, this is great. By the end we were really into it, we were out there dancing with them. But getting up for school the next day was rough.

Bay City Rollers, of course, which when you look back is an embarrassment. I had the short trousers, which I made, then put the tartan on the bottom, and the big platforms.

All the way through the fads, there was always soul music. I wasn't into disco, but you always had Stevie Wonder, it was an underlying theme that's survived.

We loved Marc Bolan. My best friend cried and cried and cried when he died. She stayed over that night and cried all night.

When glam rock came in, you insisted on watching *Top of the Pops* on Thursday night mainly to enrage your father, because there'd be men with make-up on. If you got your dad and your granddad in the same room you got double score. They couldn't understand what was going on at all.

The King is dead

I was in Corfu when I heard Elvis was dead. I was amazed, because you didn't expect Elvis to die. And I remember thinking at the time, oh, this is going to be my President Kennedy thing: I'll always remember where I was when I heard Elvis had died.

Marc Bolan's an ''Electric Warrior'. Marc Bolan is T.Rex Marc Bolan is in SOUNDS this week . . . in full colour.

Marc Bolan . . . . . . is the subject of an exclusive interview. That's not all. There are many other features, news and reviews. in SOUNDS. And there are free albums. And £400 of Laney amplification to be won. All in...

sounds
AND YET IT'S ONLY 6p

Elvis's death had an enormous impact on me, I bawled my eyes out for about two days. He'd been a hero of my childhood. I'd always wanted to be Elvis, which would have been tricky, given that I'm female. Naturally, I wanted to be the young rebellious Elvis, not the fat old Elvis.

I cried in my bed at the death of Elvis, because it coincided with my doing crap at A-levels. I just thought, this is the way life is going to be, it's going to be downhill. This is it.

It was very sad. I remember sitting outside the house in my boyfriend's car, with Radio Luxembourg on, and the announcer came on and said, The King is dead. My whole body had this awful tremor through it, I went all cold.

HOW TO SPOT THE TELL-TALE SIGNS

HOW CAN YOU SPOT IF YOUR CHILD IS READING 'SNIFFING GLUE?' —see page 8

PARENTS ARE the people who know least about the habits of *SG Readers*. And yet they should be playing a vital role in the fight to stamp it out.

So what are the signs they should be looking for? This is the question we put to Dr Mary Gardner of Lanarkshire Health board.

She said parents should look for a staggering walk and a glazed look about the eyes.

The *SG Reader* undergoes massive mood swings. "He can be very cheerful at one time and depressed and withdrawn at another. This all depends on whether or not he is under the influence of a *SG*," said Dr Gardner.

He often locks himself away in his room. There is a desire to isolate himself during the hangover stage which can be very severe. He can also be sick.

SG Readers tend to go off their food and are listless. Their hair, breath, clothing and bedrooms also small of the *SG* being used. The *SG's* leave stains on clothes and this is another telltale sign.

Dr Gardner advises that parents should speak to the child about their suspicions and if proved correct consult the family doctor for advice.

QUOTE

'Parents must be told about the dangers so that they can help the young people.' Dr Gardner.

1977'S ANSWER TO THE BIBLE... HONEST

SNIFFIN' GLUE...
AND OTHER ROCK'N'ROLL

ITS, FOR HUMANS

the brutal reality

ISSUE 6 NOW OUT.
WITH PISTOLS, GEN X, CHELSEA + EATE

these old men, who I could hardly see, singing songs about a place I'd never been, and about a lifestyle I couldn't imagine – it was all about deserts and hot sun, and I grew up in industrial Staffordshire. I remember sitting there feeling such an intense disappointment. Not long afterwards, I was going out with a boy called Earl, an American, who worked in a record shop at the weekends. I went to his house one night in November 1976 and he said, This single came in today by a new band. You've got to hear it. And he played me 'Anarchy in the UK'. And I just remember it was like St Paul for me. It finished, and he said, It's pretty cool, isn't it? They're called the Sex Pistols. I just said, Shut up and play it again. The next day I went out and bought it. That Thursday I bought *New Musical Express* and they were on the front. I had all my hair cut off, I had spiky hair. Overnight, I went from a long-haired California wannabe in a denim dress to a punk rocker. It was this wonderful moment of hearing something that related to *me*.

Along came punk

I think all decades hinge in the middle. And there was a definitive hinge for me in 1976, when I was sixteen. I'd been mad about pop music all my life, but it defined me totally as a teenager. And I went to see the Eagles: the band of California, the West Coast sound band, living totally in the sixties. It was one of those giant concerts. I remember clearly what I wore: I had on a faded denim dress with poppers up the front, and boots, and I had long blonde hair parted in the middle. And about half a mile away on the stage were

What punk gave me, apart from an outlet for my teenage nihilism and great music – I mean, the Sex Pistols were really great, that music still does it for me, The Clash still do it for me – was a community. Suddenly, I had a community. My friends were all in dead-end jobs, but one of them had a car and we would drive to Birmingham, which was an hour's drive, to see bands. I saw all the big bands, including the Sex Pistols. They were amazing, so *not* disappointing.

My friend was in a really serious punk scene in the King's Road in 1978. They were followers of Adam Ant, just when he was beginning to become known, playing in pubs. We'd thought punk was over; the Sex Pistols had split up, it had become part of the scenery. *The Two Ronnies* would do punk sketches, that kind of thing. We'd hang out in this pub called The Roebuck. Once Johnny Lydon came in, and we saw the Sex Pistols again when they were making the film *The*

Great Rock 'n' Roll Swindle. It was an amazing scene down there. Everyone in the King's Road wanted to take our photograph, and we'd demand money for it.

Every single night, we'd go to clubs or pubs, we'd go all over London. I remember amazing parties in disused factories and things. It was anarchy. Somebody would tell us there was a party at such and such a place, and we'd just go along in this flow. There was always something to go to.

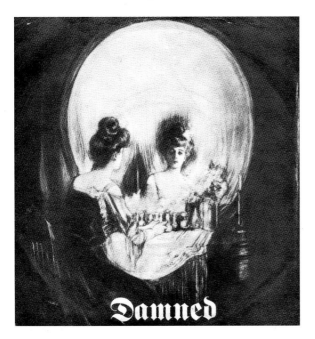

When the punk thing came in I thought, What on earth is going on here, why do people like this stuff? But after a while I got the hang of it and realized there was a fun element to it. A lot of it was quite tongue in cheek and deliberately throwaway. It was quite refreshing. It's still good to listen to.

I got into punk a bit. I went to see The Jam in Leeds, at the Students' Union there. It was the first time I'd been among real punks, and it was pretty terrifying. Everyone had spiky hair and dog collars and Mohicans. I had a safety pin through my ear.

We got a copy of 'God Save the Queen', and we thought that was a big emblem, to have a copy of a banned record.

A boy I knew was in a punk band. He had spiky blond hair, and he'd dye it pink or green or leopard spots. He used to go down to the local butcher's and get all the offal. We'd go and see him playing and he'd throw all this offal around, spray blood around the stage and into the audience. It was really gross. Not at all hippie, no peace and love there!

The big thing in the seventies for me was punk rock. I used to go up to the Hope and Anchor in Islington to watch a band called Nine Nine Nine, who I expected to be huge. But they weren't, they disappeared. But I do remember seeing The Damned at Wardour Street. The lead singer was always dressed Dracula-like. I was standing at the back, and I remember seeing this great shower of spit going up, and afterwards a great gob of it hanging from his nose. I thought, well, this is different.

All that pogoing, and the ripped clothes. I found all that anarchic stuff quite liberating. I was really into glam rock in my early teens – Bowie and Roxy Music, which was a bit of an evolution from the hippie sixties thing – but punk rock was a complete revolution. It was all these people going 'fuck you'. Which was great.

For the Queen's Silver Jubilee in 1977, we were all at my parents' beach house in Wales. There was a whole group of families, we'd all grown up together and I did absolutely love it, but by then I was a full-blown punk. We were having this middle-class barbecue outside, and I played 'God Save the Queen' by the Sex Pistols. It had the ideal effect, it really pissed everybody off.

Concerts

I went to the Isle of Wight Festival in 1970 with a couple of schoolfriends, the one Jimi Hendrix played at. I'd seen him at the Marquee in about 1967, and I'd been interested in his music ever since. We got a train down to Portsmouth, then got a ferry across. We didn't actually have tickets to get in, and we didn't pay. We were probably some of the people who pushed the wall down so we could see properly.

The first band I went to see was Slade, in 1972. My best friend and I wore fake fur bomber jackets, floral Laura Ashley-type long skirts and platform shoes. What we must have looked like …

I was fascinated by Slade. I remember going to a gig of theirs in Cornwall in '73 or '74 with my brother and pogoing like mad in this sweaty hall, and finally realizing that the guy who was pogoing behind me was actually masturbating. OK, it was my bum, because we were pogoing so closely together. I was totally outraged by this; he was getting a free ride, as it were, so I told him to stop but he just grinned stupidly. In the end, I felt so violated that I reached behind me to his crutch, grabbed him, then pogoed violently and just about ripped his bits off. He gave an unearthly squeal, but nobody noticed because everyone was squealing – this was the forerunner of the mosh pit – and then he fainted. I pogoed away to another part of the hall and let him slip to the ground and get trampled to death, I hoped.

I couldn't hear for three days after a Slade concert. You had to *feel* the noise level, because you couldn't hear it.

I was always bopping off to see Slade and Elton John, David Bowie, Hot Chocolate. We danced in the aisles. Try and stop me …

The first open-air all-weekend rock concert I went to was the Bath Festival in 1971, I think, or 1972. Four of us went in an old Volkswagen, and the roads were blocked for miles around with people and vehicles descending on the site. It took hours, crawling along the country lanes, and for some reason the heater in the VW was stuck on. We nearly died of heat exhaustion, even with the windows open. But the weekend itself was wet, and fairly miserable. The food was a rip-off, the queues for toilets unbelievable, and the atmosphere was distinctly sub-Woodstock.

JOHN WALSH
Associate editor of the *Independent*, in which he writes a column, *Tales From the City*.
Grew up in London, of Irish parents, a boyhood he later lyrically described in a memoir,
***The Falling Angels*.**

Here's a classic scene from student life in 1973/4, replicated in every student dwelling all over the nation.

It is 11.30 p.m. The pubs have shut. Nobody wants to go to bed. Everybody has popped into Dave's room, because he is the popular, elegantly wayward, Anglo-Indian scholar of the English department at my Oxford college. He is also the most reliable source of dope. He owns a Gibson redwood guitar and strums it in a vague and wispy fashion while we sit around the room making coffee. Then he shuts up because somebody has put on The Record, and an unchanging night-time ritual is about to be enacted.

The record is *Tubular Bells*, Mike Oldfield's debut and the first record launched on Richard Branson's Virgin label. Everybody, but I mean *everybody*, has got a copy. It's an hour of wibbly guitar noodling that culminates in a single phrase endlessly repeated with variations, in the style of Ravel's *Bolero*. It was the music everyone played while getting stoned. Somebody was always skinning up in a corner – packet of Marlboro or Rothmans, pack of orange Rizla papers, bits of torn cardboard for the 'roach' – the end you stuck between your lips. Twelve of us sat around the room, dozing on cushions, chatting, taking the piss, worrying about essays (lack of inspiration), worrying about girls (lack of funds or indeed sexual appeal), and doing a lot of giggling and holding the sweet smoke inside you until you almost turned blue. It was like an opium den in there, straight from the pages of Conan Doyle.

And then this thing would happen. God, it was so typically male. At the end of *Tubular Bells* – say, ten minutes from the end – the voice of Vivien Stanshall, late of the Bonzo Dog Doodah Band, comes in from nowhere. He says, 'Grand piano' and the theme is taken up by, yes, a piano, and it wanders along for a while and Stanshall says, 'Double speed guitar' or 'Glockenspiel' or one of a dozen other instruments which take up on the theme, all multitracking away on top of each other, doing the same theme but thickening the texture all the time. And the really cool dopeheads among us would know, however stoned they were, the exact second when Stanshall's voice was going to come in and would say it along with him – 'Grand piano.' If you said it at precisely the right second, it was brilliant. If you got it wrong by half a beat, you felt unbelievably stupid. The real anoraks and Northern chemists would join in with all Stanshall's little introductions, but we thought that was a bit too eager. It was much smarter to come in on the more amusing ones, like when he says, 'Two slightly dis-torted guitars …'. And then at the end, Viv on the record and all twelve of us in the room would all say together, 'Plus – TUBULAR BELLS' and these great Notre Dame cathedral bells would sound, climactically, and we all giggled some more in our stoned way, and nobody could ever summon the energy to get up and change the record. We'd shamble off to our various beds shortly after that, well pleased with the ritual.

Tony Blair was in the year above me. I bet he had a few dozen *Tubular Bells* moments. I bet he was there in a room like that with people like that, a bit stoned and giggly. I bet if you played the album to him now, he'd know more or less where to say 'Grand piano' with Viv. Though of course I'd get there slightly before him.

Alexandra Palace was a good venue for bands, a lot of big names played there. I saw the Grateful Dead there, and Led Zeppelin twice. Then I saw Led Zeppelin again at Earls Court. I was working for CBS and I used to get free tickets, but a lot of these were for European bands that weren't very well known, quite a few Dutch bands. We'd go to places like the Speakeasy. Trouble was, none of the bands came on stage until about one in the morning, and everyone was either blind drunk or falling asleep.

Windsor Great Park had some good outdoor rock concerts in the seventies. I can't remember who played at them, though. Everyone was smoking copious amounts of cannabis resin, which doesn't always help the memory, does it?

I went to Glastonbury, but it rained, and there were five of us in a two-man tent. We just about got our heads in, and our feet were outside. It was a bit grim, really.

I remember going to one of the first big outdoor concerts in Wembley, in about 1974, to see Crosby, Stills, Nash and Young, and the Byrds, and Joni Mitchell, all in one go. It was a huge day, a lovely day in early summer. I spent all day getting slowly drunk. But my girlfriend doesn't remember anything beyond the horror of trying to get home afterwards, stuck in an enormous traffic jam.

I and a few friends at school wanted to be Bryan Ferry. We started growing our hair into a floppy bit at the front, and we'd go to see Roxy Music at the Hammersmith Odeon. I saw them six or seven times. Every time, there'd be crowds of people, hordes, wearing what he'd worn on the last album cover. He did a solo album and wore a white tuxedo with a black bow tie on the cover. So everybody turned up in white tuxes, and he turned up on stage in army gear. He did it to us every time. Next concert, we turned up in army gear and he was wearing a bright blue suit.

I saw Rod Stewart at the last-ever Buxton Pop Festival, which would have been about 1975. Family were also on, and some other quite big names. It rained, of course, the entire time.

One of the first New Wave bands I saw in concert was Eddie and the Hotrods. I thought it was like a revolution. Now I look at it and it seems like a marketing ploy, but it was very clever, taking music back to basics. The atmosphere at the concert was tremendous. Johnny Rotten – John Lydon – was in the band. I said, Oh, that's Johnny Rotten, and went over to talk to him. He had bondage gear on, and bandages and safety pins and so on, and he swore a bit, but he certainly wasn't the person we all saw on the *Grundy Show* or anything like that. It was very much, There's the person, and over there is the image.

Discos, dancing, clubs and pubs

I still love all that disco music; nothing gets me on the dance floor quicker than that funky seventies sound.

Disco was fantastic. My awakening was Gloria Gaynor's 'I Will Survive'. The Embassy nightclub opened, and Thelma Houston and all these amazing, mostly black singers happened, Sylvester and all that – funk happened.

Dancing was a big, big thing. I first learned to dance in a pub called the Dragon in Hoxton, to James Brown's 'Sex Machine'. I was taught to do these particular dance steps by a guy called John Ritchie, who was even weirder than the rest of us. He had big, big spiky hair, quite long; a Bowie clone. The next time I saw him he'd changed a little bit – he was called Sid Vicious. I thought, blimey, that's John.

We used to go to nightclubs in Harrogate when the pubs closed. This was before the drink-driving laws were enforced; we'd drive all over the place absolutely paralytic. We'd go to Number Eleven. It was so sophisticated: it had lights under the dance floor, little smoky booths.

I loved dancing. When *Saturday Night Fever* came along I thought I'd died and gone to heaven, because I just loved discos. I made my boyfriend learn the whole dance sequence from the film, all the twirling, so that we could do it on the dance floor. I bought the soundtrack and played it over and over and over again.

We'd go to Dingwall's in Camden. I remember them looking through your handbags on the way in, checking for drugs.

I used to go to the Marquee Club every other Thursday evening – they had ads in *Melody Maker* saying that if you went in before seven o'clock you could get in free. Three of us used to go. We were sixteen, seventeen, and we had to be home by eleven on the dot. So we'd get there early and leave early, and we had a great time. I saw Thin Lizzy there. We'd have one lager during the whole evening.

We tended to go to pubs in Newcastle. The only pubs worth going to were those with standing room only, and not going to one, but one after the other.

We used to go to youth club every week. We'd practise our dance, we'd stand in a line and do a sequence of movements, then on Saturday night we'd go to the club and do them with gusto. That was at a tame place in Manchester called Rotters.

I used to go to Pips, which had seven discotheques, each with a different theme ranging from the Quo to David Bowie to punk. I remember seeing the Buzzcocks and the Stranglers in the punk part.

I thought dancing was for girls and poofs. I had a couple of forward mates in the seventies who'd go out on the dance floor and dance. I thought it was bizarre. I still think it's bizarre, men dancing. I was always at the bar, getting the drinks. I stood there until I was ready to fall over, then I went home.

We had discos in the south lakes, but we were very stuck. Your father came for you at eleven o'clock and stood in the doorway with his arms folded, and that was it. Our discos were very stylized in terms of behaviour. Girls danced around their handbags, then the boys just came in for the last ten minutes, for the smoochy ones.

At school discos we'd be taught to do the square tango and the St Bernard's waltz and the veleta, and we'd be expected to perform those before we were allowed to dance to our own music. They were instilling some social graces into us.

We'd go to Sid's in Stalybridge on a Thursday night. Train for rugby, skinful of ale at the rugby club, about eleven o'clock go down to Sid's and disco on until one in the morning. But I never got away from the bar. Music? What's that noise going on? I can hardly hear myself fall over.

The easiest way to play music and see your friends in my small town was to go to each other's houses. So we'd do that. One guy's parents had a great big rambling old house and they didn't use half of it, so we were able to go there every Saturday night. It was like a club. We had all the rooms in the basement: we had a drinks room, a music room, a dark room. We'd pay 2p, just to cover the cost of the electricity – 2p! Just a token gesture, really.

The popular dance was the Mud, the Tiger Feet dance – it was great. It wasn't really a dance, you just walked, one foot in front, then across, then back. You'd all stand in a line and go forwards and across and back, like the band did it. Showaddywaddy.

At college, we spent most of our time going to big old London pubs that had been converted into disco clubs. I can remember the old pub in the King's Road, The Six Bells, which had girls dancing in cages, go-go dancers, that sort of thing.

We blokes didn't dance in the seventies. We stood and propped up the bar and looked cool. Dancing was definitely not something you did. Some of the girls would dance, and you'd dance to some of the slow songs with girls, but you never saw couples dancing the way my kids do now, or the way people danced in the sixties. It was just different.

Television and radio

We watched television a lot as a family, because we only had one set. On Saturday afternoon we'd watch *Dr Who* together, and my mother would have made a cake or scones.

In those days you just had one television in the house, and everybody sat down as a family and watched a programme. You ate in time to watch it, then you all sat down. It's so different now.

We always sat down as a family and watched things like *The Onedin Line*. It was family entertainment, and at strict times too, because you couldn't video it.

Dallas was really, seriously important. It came from another planet. We didn't have anything like it; the closest we came to that kind of glamour was Elsie Tanner.

I was fascinated by *Triangle*, the BBC's cut-price attempt to do an early-evening soap. It was absolutely hilarious. It had cardboard sets and totally preposterous scenarios. There was murder, intrigue, betrayal, lust, kidnapping – all the ingredients of high drama, but all taking place on the cross-Channel ferry from Harwich to the Hook of Holland. Any less glamorous place than a North Sea cross-Channel ferry is hard to imagine.

The Six Million Dollar Man was a big deal. I saw it again recently – God, it was awful.

Peter Wingard played Jason King, a trendy bloke who wore really flashy round-shouldered suits, and he'd have the cuffs of his shirt turned back up over the sleeve of the jacket. He had this big handlebar moustache. He was awful, just terrible.

The Golden Shot, with Bob Monkhouse. Now that was a programme we used to watch. Remember 'Bernie, the bolt'?

Budgie was fantastic. I liked Adam Faith because he had this real London, Cockney accent, and it was the first time I'd heard it on TV in a hero rather than a villain. He was so cool.

I loved all the BBC classics. When *War and Peace* was on I was in heaven. *I, Claudius* was on twice a week on BBC2 – this was way before video. Each episode was repeated, and I watched each episode twice.

My ambition for a while was to leave school and get a flat in Chelsea and be like the girls in *Man About the House* and *The Liver Birds.* That's why I went to university: to leave home and get my own place. I wanted to have fun, and be independent, and television showed me how that could be.

Because I had a sports-mad brother and father, Saturday television was football, boxing and wrestling. Even now, the theme song to *Match of the Day* fills me with the shivers because I can't bear it. They completely took over the house. Mum and I had to go the laundrette and

do the shopping while the men watched sport on television. I couldn't wait to get away.

I watched *Charlie's Angels* every Thursday night without fail. It was wonderful. My mum used to say to me, and she had a spike up her arse when she said it, Why can't I have hair like Farah Fawcett-Majors? And I'd say, Because you don't spend three hours doing it every day.

We'd watch *Charlie's Angels* every week. I can't remember any story lines except one, when Farrah Fawcett-Majors was chasing after somebody on a skateboard. It was preposterous. She was skateboarding underneath lorries and holding on to the back of them and so on, and we were all hysterical in our student house, laughing at this. Then about two years afterwards, I was driving along in my car and I heard a radio programme about a millionaire skateboard

When *Charlie's Angels* came along, I used it as a kind of religion. I went on this terrible diet and became anorexic. I remember thinking, If I lose another half-stone I'll look like Farrah Fawcett-Majors and everybody will love me.

There was a play on at nine o'clock on Saturdays called *Thriller*. It started out being called *Menace*. It always began with an American tourist who came to a picturesque Cotswold village, and you knew he was dead meat. There was always something sinister that got him in the end.

Television was absolutely fabulous in the seventies. I thought the programmes were wonderful, they were so fantastical. Things like *Randall & Hopkirk, Deceased, Tales of the Unexpected*, things that just weren't possible.

1970, the first World Cup in colour.

I'd stay in every Christmas to watch Morecambe and Wise, and I'd be ridiculed by my friends who were all at the pub. But they were so funny.

entrepreneur. They asked him where he'd got his ideas from, and he said, Well, I was watching this *Charlie's Angels* programme, and I thought, what a fantastic idea …

The Sweeney was a wonderful series. They'd wreck a Jaguar every week. It was the first programme where the police were shown to be a bit dodgy.

The first-ever colour television I got, in 1975, worked by touch. It was fascinating. It worked on the moisture in your skin when you touched it gently, to change channels. They don't exist any more. I remember once a whole lot of us sitting in my living room watching this cowboy film, and I sneezed. And it changed the channels, but it was another cowboy film, and it was about five minutes before everyone turned to each other and said, Does anyone know what's happening? Because nothing made sense. Mind you, two

television channels showing cowboy films is a sign of the times too, isn't it?

Watching *Top of the Pops* was something I had to do every week. I couldn't imagine getting to a time of life when I wouldn't watch it, without fail, every week.

Indoor League was a fantastic programme, where they did bar-top skittles, darts, dominoes, stuff like that. It always started off with, Now then. And finished with, I'll sithee. Yorkshire TV.

Thursday nights was *Top of the Pops*, followed by *Star Trek*. In college we'd have our meal at six, and on Thursday nights people would just scoff like you wouldn't believe, to run out and get to the television room and get a decent seat.

We just pissed ourselves laughing at *Derek and Clive*. We used to bring the album into school and play it, and our teachers were appalled. I think we liked it *because* our teachers were appalled.

Radio was good fun because we were getting Radio 1. Johnny Walker and Tony Blackburn.

On Sunday nights I'd sit in the bath with the transistor going, listening to the Top 20 on Radio 1. It was so important to hear the nation's number one.

Radio Luxembourg, every Tuesday night, listening to the Top 40. It would go on from eleven until one, I think, so I was always in bed, listening to my transistor under the covers so that nobody else in the house could hear it.

Monty Python

In school, whenever *Monty Python* had been on the night before, everyone would be repeating every word, going round saying 'Dinsdale' in that deep voice. We didn't have videotapes, but we could all remember every sketch, all the words, the next day.

I remember watching *Monty Python* on television one night and nearly weeping with laughter, and then immediately afterwards the news and current affairs show seemed just like an extension, equally hilarious and surreal. It was hard to tell when one ended and the other began.

I didn't always like *Monty Python*, I thought it very sexist. Even as an eleven-year-old, I found it sexist.

I could chant whole scenes from *Monty Python.*

I had to get *Monty Python* stuff second-hand off my brother the next morning, because I wasn't allowed to stay up and watch it.

Films

It was a good decade for films. One that had a big impact on me was *Clockwork Orange*. It came out when I was about thirteen, but it wasn't out for long because it got banned by Kubrick. I bunked in to see it at Hackney Odeon. I found something incredibly attractive about it, although I wasn't a particularly violent person.

We had a flea-pit cinema in our town, and from the age of thirteen onwards I went to see every single film. I went to see *Easy Rider* every night for a week. It changed my life. I still love it. It was a sixties film, but it's stayed OK. The freedom of it; I got obsessed with America through this film. I thought they were so cool, those guys.

American cinema in the seventies was so incredible. I look back on it now and I marvel at *Butch Cassidy and the Sundance Kid*, and *Apocalypse Now*, which was the last great seventies film.

I went to the first night of *Saturday Night Fever* and I thought it was wonderful, a great film.

The Deer Hunter was such an amazing film. It was all very shaping, and consciousness-raising. Until then

I'd always seen America as this benign, fabulous source of everything stylish; now I saw the other side of it, starting with *Serpico*. Anything with Al Pacino or Robert De Niro in; they were my gods.

I was at the première of *The Buddy Holly Story* the night Keith Moon died.

Do you remember *Deep Throat*? I have a friend who got hold of a copy and had a Sunday afternoon showing. We had a snack break in the middle, when she had to change reels, and she served bloody great sausages. No one could eat them.

I remember going to see *Grease* with a friend. We thought it was great, and that John Travolta was really cool. He was, and he is again.

I saw *Grease* many times. I loved anything to do with John Travolta – still do!

I wrote this critique in my 1978 diary: 'Went to see *Saturday Night Fever*. The dancing and the clothes were fantastic, but the plot and the structure lacked.' I can't believe I was clever enough to write that. Because the next entry is: 'Went to the Steak and Fish Inn in town with Keith. Mum liked him, but that's not saying much when you consider that she thinks my dad is fanciable.'

The seventies were a low point for film-goers. We all saw through the cardboard sets of the disaster movies. The Bond films were the only things worth seeing until Spielberg got going. I watched *Live and Let Die*, which was the first Roger Moore Bond film, sixteen or seventeen times.

PARAMOUNT PICTURES PRESENTS

The Godfather

The *Oz* trial was an influence on me at the beginning of the seventies, and Pasolini's *Requiem*. As a rite of passage, I'd just seen *Seventeen* and *Here We Go Round the Mulberry Bush*, Hunter Davies's novel transformed into our idea of the good life.

My girlfriend absolutely hated *Clockwork Orange*. I bought the LP, the soundtrack, and it was quite unusual for the time because it had 'The Thieving Magpie' on it, and 'Singing in the Rain'.

I saw *Clockwork Orange* when it came out and I thought it was the sickest thing. It's up there – or rather, down there – in my mind with that awful Susan George film, *Straw Dogs*. And it was so chillingly prescient, wasn't it?

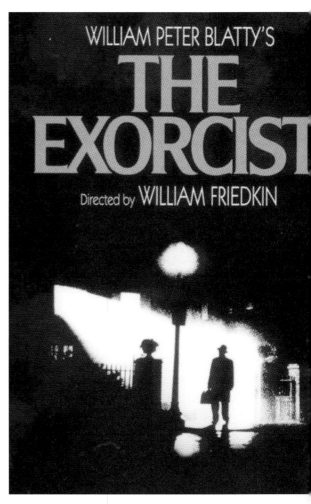

I thought *Clockwork Orange* was really good. I don't think it glorified violence. But it did worry me that when I went to see it, there were people coming out of the previous showing dressed up like the blokes in the film. That was awful.

I remember *Women in Love*. Oliver Reed and Alan Bates wrestling naked in front of the fire … I was heavily taken with that. But they were still making *Carry On* films, which typified what was going on in British culture at that time.

I laughed all the way through *Jaws*, and people were really outraged.

I found *The Exorcist* quite disturbing, more so than I'd have admitted at the time. Also *Clockwork Orange*. Some of the blokes at school started wearing some of the gear, and I found it very sad, how people could be influenced.

Magazines and newspapers

Harry Evans and his *Sunday Times* are the reason I'm a journalist today. My father was a voracious reader of newspapers, and the *Sunday Times* magazine had the most amazing photography, such as a portfolio by Don McCullin of the Vietnam War: pictures of people having their heads blown off and stuff. Which I think was very important for me to see. And then you'd turn the page and there'd be a piece about Roxy Music or someone, with fabulous colour pictures. And because I loved the magazine so much I started to read the paper. I remember my father laughing out loud at one of Clive James's columns, so I read it, and then I would read it every week, then I'd read anything Katherine Whitehorn wrote, and I just got drawn into this world. The *Sunday Times* in the seventies was a fantastic newspaper. The fact that it could appeal to a thirteen-year-old girl as well as her parents was pretty amazing.

I didn't really understand *Nova* because I was too young, but I knew it was special. And I loved Molly Parkin's fashion pages.

I remember the *Oz* trial. My brother had the magazine, so I saw it before the trial started, and I remember thinking, this is saucy! But I didn't think anything more of it, so I was amazed when it came to trial.

I started my own punk fanzine called *Punkture* and I had a punk name, I was called Pretty Nasty. We used to photocopy *Punkture* and staple it together. My friend Paula and I were the editors and we'd write the articles and cut photographs out of *NME* or whatever and literally glue them in. Then we'd photocopy them and sell them to record shops and at gigs. It was quite successful, and really good fun.

I didn't read serious newspapers; I don't think I ever picked one up. Newspapers weren't around in my house – except for the *News of the Screws*. Isn't that weird? I did block release journalism, and when I was at college they brought out a *News of the Screws* item on a headmaster in the north of England who had advertised in a swingers magazine, and they found him in some orgy and outed him, and he killed himself. This was brought up in a course on responsible journalism: he'd been a single man, surely he wasn't doing anything wrong? It was the first time it had occurred to me that maybe the *News of the Screws* wasn't the great newspaper I thought it was.

I remember knowing the day the new *Cosmopolitan* was due out. I'd go to the newsagent on the way home from school and buy the new issue and just drink it up. All those staged shots of beautiful people having fun. It was just another world, it was so sophisticated.

Cosmo was it for me. I saw all these wonderful women with beautiful hair and beautiful smiles and briefcases, sitting behind desks, and that was me, that's what I wanted to be. And I think that's why boys never pinned me down. I was always the one that did the leaving.

There was a fantastic publication called *Speed and Power* when I was about fourteen. It was all about Second World War aircraft, racing cars; the centre spread would be a Lancaster bomber or an XR71. There'd be an Arthur C. Clarke or an Isaac Asimov science fiction story every week. It was brilliant, but it went bust.

CARMEN CALLIL
Australian feminist who founded, in 1972, the publishing house Virago, run by women to produce books written by women. Later became boss of Chatto and Windus; now a writer herself and a regular book reviewer for the *Daily Telegraph*.

In 1971 I had given up being a wage slave in book publishing and was working for *Ink*, the newspaper which Richard Neville, Andrew Fisher and Ed Victor had launched as a bridge between the underground press (*Oz* and *IT*) and the Fleet Street newspapers where life centred on El Vino's, a bar where I spent much of the 1960s and 70s. It had taken time to get myself together after arriving from Australia with a one-way ticket to a colder and stranger world. Women's liberation had already reached Britain in 1970, by way of the USA and Germaine Greer, who came from the same beach suburbs of Melbourne as myself, and whose book *The Female Eunuch* I happened to publicize when I was working for her publisher. I took to it like a duck to water, or rather to certain parts of the large lake it turned out to be.

I had spent lovely years in the 60s working for publishers, all men, all leftish, all sweethearts really but given to long boozy lunches and not much work. When I got to *Ink* it was much the same: lots of rather useless but seriously divine men, being not very good at what they were doing: but then they had to contend with the *Oz* trial, and poor *Ink* didn't get much of a look-in. I can do better than this, I thought (I was wrong). In those days, you felt anybody could do anything.

I'd been wearing hot-pants for years already. One of my employers later told me that they gave me the job because I turned up for my 1967 interview wearing a pair of them in bright red corduroy. I did not wear these when I went to ask the bank for an overdraft to start Virago; I wasn't that stupid.

Starting Virago was simply marvellous fun. I would change the world by publishing books which celebrated women and women's lives, and thus spread the message of women's liberation to the whole population and knock on the head forever the idea that it was anything to do with burning bras or hating men. I always believed that books, writers, changed lives, and I still believe it.

I lived off the King's Road in an attic bedsitter above a synagogue, and on Saturdays the chant from below mixed with the noise of Carly Simon's 'You're So Vain' from the record shops. Ossie Clark's shop was at the end of my street and I wore his scanty flowing numbers as I pottered up and down the street exuding style and commitment. Not just to women and what women did but to everything that might change the world. I canvassed for Wilson, raised money for Bangladesh, marched, and staged a union demo in Trafalgar Square. (They gave me a lighter as a thank-you present, which I still have.)

Women surged up the steep stairs to my attic, some of them angry women. Why did I give my women's publishing company such an aggressive, man-hating name, they wanted to know. Irony, I would reply. Others toiled upstairs with manuscripts on Russian women revolutionaries, ancient goddesses, interviews with women famous and unknown, children, motherhood, cancer. Can I help? they would say. And all of them did, hundreds of women helped me start Virago. Little did we know that despite all the good things about it – and there were some very good things in its heyday – it also led to the first murmurs of Margaret Thatcher, who became Tory leader in 1975, and the first woman prime minister in 1979. Not the heroine we had been working towards. But she was only one woman. There were millions of others like me, whose lives were changed by the feminism of the 1960s and 70s; and the lives of our brothers, uncles, fathers were changed too.

WILKO EXITS FEELGOODS

Sacked, or did he sack himself! Pages 3 & 11

BIG COLOUR PIN-UP OF ELVIS THURSDAYS 3½p

No. 450 AUGUST 19th 1972

Jackie

YOU'RE INTO SOMETHING GOOD !

No. 377 MARCH 27th, 1971 THURSDAYS 3½p

Jackie

brings you the magic of spring love

I shared *New Musical Express* with my friend, who bought *Melody Maker*. That formed our opinion. I thought I was a cut above the rest because I got *NME. Melody Maker* was for the plebs.

We were a *Daily Mirror* household. My political thoughts were formed by my father, who told me that the likes of us don't vote Tory.

I was an absolutely committed *Guardian* reader in the seventies; I'd never have thought then that I'd ever read anything else.

Katherine Whitehorn in the *Observer,* Hunter Davies in *Punch*, writing feature pieces in a totally new way. Instead of writing about the great and the good, they were writing about staying with your friends and discovering your child cleaning between its toes with your host's electric toothbrush. Those things as ideas for articles hadn't been done before.

The *BIT* guides became my bibles in the seventies, when I started travelling. They were brilliant.

Jackie all the way

I was addicted to *Jackie* in my early teens. The stories were all the same, and either had a happy ending, when the boy and girl got together for ever after, or a sad ending, in which case the last two drawings were the boy walking off into the sunset and the girl

sitting with tears in her eyes saying, 'Red was a loner'. I'd feel sad all through Maths.

When *Jackie* arrived I'd scuttle upstairs with it and get back into bed and go straight to the 'Dear Claire' page at the end. 'Dear Claire, I have a terrible problem … I cannot get a boyfriend. Please tell me how.' And I'd read on, thinking, how, how, how?

My room was wallpapered in *Jackie* posters. It was a great, great magazine. *Jackie* was *the* seventies magazine. And it always had great offers, so you had to buy it: a free make-up bag, or a free comb, or the latest gizmo.

On the day *Jackie* magazine came out, we used to sit on the desks at school with our feet on the chairs and read the problem page and find out how to kiss boys.

Books
If anyone was essential, it was Germaine Greer – an antidote to all the crap, someone with intelligence and vision and courage. And Angela Phillips – *Our Bodies Ourselves*.

Erich von Däniken, *Chariots of the Gods*. Suddenly there was all this kind of mystic voodoo stuff, where do we come from, *Supernature* and so on. And warning books:

The Secret Life of Plants, Recipe for a Small Planet. They had been around before, but the whole thing became huge in the seventies.

I read Jean-Paul Sartre's *Age of Reason* and it really freaked me out; it was all so desperate, so, well, existentialist. Really depressing. I got so depressed I couldn't stop crying.

We really got into Oscar Wilde at my school. There was a craze for those Oscar Wilde put-downs, bang, just like that, a witty or nasty rejoinder. It became a real pain in the bum after a while.

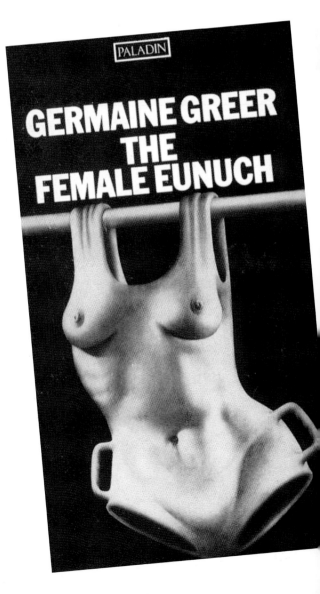

OUR BODIES OURSELVES

a health book by and for women

Boston Women's Health Book Collective
British edition by Angela Phillips and Jill Rakusen

First British Edition Fully Revised

I can remember sitting reading *The Female Eunuch* and one of my male flatmates picking it up and sneering at it. He happened to open it at a page which discussed the implications of dressing baby boys in blue and baby girls in pink. He was so contemptuous and dismissive. I sat there in an inarticulate rage, unable to counter his arguments but knowing that he was so wrong. There was still very much a sneering attitude then, which doesn't exist today. Men today are either for or agin, but they don't treat the subject as if it had the importance and significance of a knitting pattern.

I didn't read any contemporary literature at all; my education was steeped in the classics.

I remember reading *The Female Eunuch*, and that was it. I was out of there.

I began to read Kate Millett. It was all very American, that women's lib stuff, but it was filtering through, it was having an effect.

Hermann Hesse, *Steppenwolf* and *The Glass Bead Game*. They were a bit of a hangover from the hippie late sixties. Those, and the Carlos Castaneda books. They really made you feel connected to the counterculture, or what was left of it.

The seventies were when I had to read things like *The School for Scandal*, Anouilh, Beckett and so on, books to study, and it took me a long time to get out of that really, and start reading for pleasure.

Hermann Hesse
The Glass Bead Game

A new translation of **Magister Ludi** by Richard and Clara Winston

The Lifestyle

Daily life in the seventies

Social experimentation and the hangover from the sixties meant that life for teenagers in the seventies was radically different in many ways from previous decades. Schools went comprehensive, there was a massive increase in college and university intake, jobs dried up, vegetarian diets came in, the squatting movement began and the sexual revolution rolled on. But some things remain timeless: teenagers experimented with sex and with substances, got their first cars, sometimes even got married – just as they always have. So much of the fabric of our daily lives changed in subtle, incremental ways. Lots of seemingly trivial innovations added up to a fundamental shift in the way things were organized.

Secondary school

When my older brother and sister went to our local school in the sixties it was quite a good grammar school, but by the time I got there it was a comprehensive with 1200 pupils and it was absolute crap. My education was crap, and I was bored. There were very few after-school activities, and I was so keen on art and music and drama: no outlet for them at all. Nothing. I was bored by the other students. I didn't fit in there, I was posh. I had to develop two different voices, one for home and one for school, so as not to be bullied. I thought tech would have more interesting people, and it did, because there were more middle-class kids there. It was a class thing more than anything. I don't think you can underestimate the power of the English class system to make you feel uncomfortable.

I went to a grammar school in East London, one of these voluntary-aided things, called Parmenter's. You had to pass your 11-plus at a certain level to get into it, which was good. It was a good school. We did Latin and the masters wore mortarboards and gowns. In the middle of East London it was very odd. We used to get picked on by the secondary school boys, because you had to wear your cap, and there were a few fights. But I was always very grateful for the chance to go to that school.

Teaching was very much a passion for teachers then. We had wonderful teachers, and lots of after-school activities – classics clubs, where we spoke only Latin, things like that. It was a very stimulating environment.

In 1970 I was sixteen and still at school in Wolverhampton, which was a dreadful experience. I was a working-class boy at a grammar school. I was the first member of my family to go through to do A-levels. In the late seventies I came across an article by David Hargreaves, an educationalist, called 'The experience of working-class boys in grammar schools'. When I read it, it was just like, Hey, that's me there. The snobbishness of the teachers. I have an accent, which I haven't lost. The school was very middle-class, and I wasn't. My headmaster told me not to apply for university. I've felt fairly bitter at some points. But I was no rebel, and I was really good at schoolwork, which means they can't touch you for it.

GCEs and CSEs. God knows why they put us in the same subjects for a GCE and a CSE, because they were two totally different syllabuses, but they did. It was like doing twelve subjects as opposed to six.

I hated my secondary school. It was rough, and there was no discipline there. I like discipline and I wanted to learn, so I didn't fit in. There was no uniform, and I always felt very uneasy about going into school wearing ordinary casual clothes.

At the time when my friends from the estate I'd grown up with were out looking for work or working, I went to sixth form and had to wear a uniform. But I found that liberating, because I didn't have to think about what I was going to wear. I also found the intelligence of my peers refreshing. I had to struggle to catch up with them, and it was a challenge.

My school went on strike. Typical of the seventies: go in and enrol, get your tie, leave. I remember going in, and *Look North-West* was outside the gates filming these pupils as they went in then immediately came out again.

I had a very poor education. You were never expected to do homework. If I was ever given homework, that was just a joke. You didn't even have to work in class. The boys didn't, anyway.

I went to a school with a very elderly staff who could remember teaching my mother. My year was the first in the county of Lancashire – Cumbria as it was – that didn't have to sit the 11-plus. My school was a former secondary modern, and it wasn't very ambitious. The grammar school was in Ulverston, and the boys there played rugby union and went on to university. My school played rugby league. Your career choice was Vickers shipyard, or something nice if you were a girl, to tide you over until you were married. They finished you off for a working life, not for a life that continued in education. So when I transferred to the sixth form in Ulverston it was a huge cultural shock.

School was a good time, because the children came from all the little villages around into one big place. There were six children in my year, sixteen in the whole school. We weren't taught sport as such, but we could dab up becks, climb trees, make spears. Why ever would you want to play a game with rules? You made your own up. It must have been like trying to educate semi-savages.

I led a very cloistered existence, I went to public school for the sons of medical gentlemen, and I was a scholarship boy. It was a place where the most outrageous act you could do was wear coloured socks.

I went to a boys' secondary modern school, which was quite strict, but I enjoyed my time there. I'd been to a very poor primary school; I was very lazy and they just let me do nothing. The secondary modern school pulled me up. It should have been a comprehensive school by then, but our council kept changing from Labour to Tory and back again, and we got to be comprehensive quite late.

JONATHAN COE

Former *Guardian* journalist, whose sixth novel, *The Rotters' Club*, is set in the seventies, in Birmingham, where he was brought up. Earlier novels won several prizes.

When I look again at my sixth-form diaries, what emerges is an unknowingly comic self-portrait of a teenager living a blissfully self-absorbed life, whose boundaries extended no further than homework, television and a fast-expanding record collection. An aspiring composer then, I was quite capable of making the po-faced announcement on February 11, 1977 that 'I gave much thought today to contemporary modern music.' What this frenzy of cogitation produced, the diaries don't record. Blanketed by an entirely stable and supportive family life, I seem to have breezed through those years in a dream world, untouched by the distant rumble of racial tensions, ideological stand-offs and bitter industrial disputes that make up the political history of the 1970s.

Yet in spite of this, something of the distinctive flavour of the decade rises up from these scribbled pages. The legions of hirsute musicians whose solemn concept albums and never-ending twiddly instrumentals we all used to discuss with such passion. The belief that to spend two weeks in a caravan in windswept north Wales was as good as a holiday could possibly get. The sense that a meal out in a Berni Inn was the height of sophistication. Like my seventeen-year-old self, the nation hadn't yet woken up to the narrowness of its horizons and learnt to laugh about them. It was an era entirely devoid of irony.

These days, of course, irony is absolutely *de rigueur* when looking back on the 1970s. We reminisce about Pan's People and sticky-back-plastic and congratulate ourselves on being so much wiser now. But there's a difference between wisdom and mere knowingness, and there's no clear evidence that the cooler, slicker, glossier culture we have created since then is any real improvement.

My high school days were really, really happy days. Although of course, even within the comprehensive system you were carefully channelled off into sets, so you were with the same thirty or forty children all the time. You weren't actually mixing and meeting with other sets.

My school was really strict. I used to get slippered for things like being the last to get changed after PE. I got hit with a cricket bat for cheating at cross-country. In technical drawing, we got the cane for dropping a pencil. You were supposed to take your punishment.

I was the second comprehensive intake in my secondary school. The classes were streamed, and it worked directly on ability. It was the PEAK DISTRICT. The PEA was known as the grammar school strain; it was a comprehensive school, so it went down to T, where you were known as a laughing stock. Nobody was supposed to know, because it was spelt PEAK DISTRICT as opposed to ABC, but of course it was so obvious.

My school, a comprehensive, gave me a lot of opportunities I wouldn't otherwise have had. I went to America on a school exchange programme; we'd go orienteering; some lads went sailing. The health and safety risks stop us from doing a lot of that now.

You still got a clip round the earhole from teachers in those days.

I didn't enjoy school particularly. And I think if you don't enjoy school, which is a big part of your life, it can colour everything. The comprehensive system started and I was the first year, the guinea-pig year, of that. I found it a great struggle. There were a lot of destructive children in the class.

There were some very rough people at my school, lots of girl gangs that I just didn't get along with. I found it all very difficult to handle. We had very big classes and I was just lost, I suppose, looking back. Lost in the system. I'd have been better in a smaller environment, but it wasn't an option.

I was terrified of the 11-plus, then I gave a big sigh of relief because I didn't have to take it. Later, I wished I had.

Everything that our parents had went into my and my brother's education. They never went out for a meal, because every penny they had went to paying for our private school, to buy the privileges that they hadn't had. So I now speak with a received pronunciation, which allows me to masquerade, to pass easily among the middle and upper classes without mistake. At school I called even my best friend by his surname.

Ours was a very strict, very conventional, very unadventurous girls' school. A single-sex direct-grant school. The English teacher was a bit of a hero in that she started to acknowledge girls as people, which was a sharp turnaround.

I thought Clydebank High School looked like a prison when I first saw it. It had brown gravel football pitches around it, and lots of graffiti

sprayed around the ground floor. Wire-mesh covers on the windows. I took one look and said, I'm not going there! But in fact it was a very good school. I liked it very much.

I was quite strictly regimented at my high school. They had the strap there, so if you stepped out of line you got a strap across the wrist, which was a bit of a shock for me.

I found my teachers inspiring, a lot of them were quite fired by what they did, particularly the Maths teachers.

My secondary school uniform was basically black or grey. My mother wouldn't let me wear black, she said no eleven-year-old girl should wear black, so I had to wear grey. Nobody wore grey, all my friends wore black. It was really awful. I sneaked the money to buy a pair of black trousers and had to hide them in my locker.

We had a Miss Watford Girls' Grammar School contest, and I was runner-up, wearing my cork platform clogs. I got a box of Maltesers.

Do you remember the huge craze for Klackers? Two rigid pieces of plastic that you clacked together. They were banned at my school because some people cracked their wrists clacking them.

My girls' grammar school was a very dark, miserable, serious time. I was very large and lived in a huge old house, and all the other girls seemed tiny and they all lived in tiny modern houses. I felt a terrible surge of inadequacy.

I went to school in Fulham. In my last year, the school was amalgamated with three other schools into Pimlico Comprehensive, which opened in 1970. It was an absolute disaster. It was appalling – a good idea that went

wrong. Two grammar schools amalgamated with one of the best technical schools of its

time, with all the equipment, and a secondary modern, and the kids didn't get on. The grammar school kids were bored, the boys from the tech complained about the workshops and the labs, and some of the secondary modern kids were out of their depth academically. It was just chaos.

Do you remember when those wicker baskets were all the rage, with the plastic panniers? They had to ban them from school, because they kept giving the parquet flooring woodworm.

My school had a ten-mile sponsored walk we went on every year. It was talked about from September, and it didn't happen until May. It was which group you were going to be in, who was going to sponsor you, what you were going to wear. I planned what I was going to wear for about four months. I was going to wear my Levis, with my Green Flash trainers – they were like the Reeboks of their day – and a cream cheesecloth shirt with one of those ties at the waist. I had a denim hat with a floppy bit with badges sewn on it – in fact I've still got it, my daughter wears it. And I planned it and planned it, and we were all in these groups. It was all who fancied who, and where you were going to have your picnic, and what you had in your picnic lunch. It was such a big deal. And on that ten-mile walk, my periods started.

After I left my voluntary-aided grammar school, the Labour Party basically put paid to grammar schools, saying this is elitist. And this made me Tory for a long time. I hated the Labour Party for doing that because it was a fantastic opportunity for an East London boy who wouldn't have that opportunity otherwise. The only people who could afford that were rich people, because they paid to go to private schools. And by banning voluntary-aided schools like mine, these working-class kids got lumped in with the rest of the slum secondary school system, which was falling apart. It was so shortsighted.

College days

At tech I did English, Psychology and Environmental Studies – it was the first year for the two latter subjects for A-levels. My Psychology tutor was a great influence on me. He was just like *The History Man* – even down to having affairs with two of his students, one of whom was me.

I went to St Andrews University as a punk, with my hair bleached white. It gave me great social cachet, because it's a very conservative, upper-class university. I hadn't been exposed to the upper classes at all. I was middle to upper middle, and so it was very confusing for me, to go from this comprehensive school where I'd been bullied for being posh, to suddenly feeling like I was dead common because I hadn't been to the right school. But I got invited to all the good dinner parties, and got in with the in-crowd. Then I didn't want to be a punk any more.

I went to Oxford, and we used to have tea parties at university all the time. It was such an easy and cheap way to entertain people. It was seventies in that you sat on the floor, and you drank out of earthenware mugs; I don't want you to think it was all bone china or anything.

I used to have money left over from my grant at the end of each year. In my last year I got £447, and I had £8 left at the end.

I was pushed into going to university, basically. I'd only just returned from hitching across Europe four days before. I remember being put on a coach at Victoria Station, and I didn't even know where Warwick was. My mum and dad had bought me a new pair of jeans. I remember them waving, and off I went. My dad was so proud, I was the first person in our family to go to university. And none of us knew where Warwick was. I thought, what the hell am I doing, where am I going? But it was exciting.

Next time you have a sit-in **get hold of the facts**

PAN books **COLES NOTES**

Coles Notes, a series of critical commentaries, have the facts *and* they are easy to digest—they all include step-by-step plot analyses and discussions, detailed character studies and biographical notes on the authors and sections dealing with each books' historical and sociological background.

Next time you 'sit-in' to study for your examinations make sure you have the Coles Notes on your subject and get your facts straight.

Among the many subjects covered are Shakespeare, Chaucer, other classics of English literature, and the General Sciences.

Send for your FREE copy of our complete list and order form, to:—
COLES NOTES DIVISION, PAN BOOKS LIMITED
33 TOTHILL STREET, LONDON, S.W.1.

NAME

ADDRESS

TOWN   COUNTY
REF:S/9/10/69

VICTORIA WOOD
Comedy actress, began appearing in the late 1970s as a standup comic. Writes her own scripts, songs and TV dramas (notably *Pat and Margaret*, for herself and Julie Walters). Her tours are sellouts and she's voted the person most people want to live next door to.

Autumn 1971 was my first term at Birmingham University – the miners' strike. I remember being in my bedsitter, in bed at nine o'clock in the evening, a power cut, candles too expensive, listening to *The Organist Entertains* on the radio my mother had got me with Green Shield stamps – feeling I wasn't perhaps getting as much out of being a student as I might.

It should have been a time of great hope and optimism, but there was a definite feeling that the sun had gone in. I blame it on the maxi-coat. I had a dark green PVC maxi-coat which had cost something unbelievable like twelve quid and I looked like a bottle bank. All the second-years wore long black skirts, blouses with huge sleeves and long petal-shaped collars with black tank-tops over, very gloomy. You needed to be very pretty indeed not to look like someone with a very small part in *Upstairs, Downstairs*.

I remember feeling a bit out of it, because I'd never managed to get through *The Female Eunuch*, though everyone had it. I could also never roll a joint, though I saw enough rolled, usually on the back of an LP, usually *Tubular Bells*.

After decimalization: one minute everything had cost two bob (i.e. 10 pence) and life was quite manageable, then suddenly everything in the shop was 37$\frac{1}{2}$p, and we all had this sense that it had all gone out of control. For years I felt I would never be able to have a car or a mortgage, because I'd never be able to keep up with inflation. I remember some oil crisis having a knock-on effect on the manufacture of vinyl, and thinking 'There goes my record career.'

The whole period was scary and unsettling. You couldn't be sure of a job, or a house, your rubbish might not get taken away, your granddad might not get buried, and if your house caught fire someone in the army might come or they might not. And when the telly went off at ten you had better just go to bed, but you better not have a baby because that would put an intolerable strain on the NHS.

I played at the Round House in John Cage's Music Circus. I had to play seventeen seconds of silence on the piano. I can now reveal I played seventeen seconds of Mrs Mills' silence and didn't bother with John Cage at all.

One of my best memories is going on television for the first time in 1974, on a local programme on BBC Birmingham which went out at 10.30 in the evening, and being thrilled the next day to be recognized in a shop. And going on *New Faces* and being told by Clifford Davies: 'This girl is very good, but she'll never work.' Oh, thanks.

My grammar school, Kingsbury County, was one of the first schools in London to offer Sociology as a GCE subject. My dad was proud that I was going to university, but he didn't know what Sociology was. I don't think he ever did find out. I wasn't all that sure myself at first, but I knew it was modern, and new, and it sounded marvellous. And we did Women's Studies, it was marvellous. Germaine Greer was at Warwick University, but she left the year I went. I could have wept. People would go to her lectures even though they weren't doing Sociology.

Starting university was peculiar for me. I had absolutely no idea what it was going to be like. Not a clue. Some of the strands of things that were surprising were the number of people from public schools. I was stupid, I should have known that, but I just didn't know. I can remember the first person I became friends with, on our first day. And what we had in common was, we both had a tie in our pocket when we turned up. Jeans on, long hair, but a tie just in case. We had no family history of that at all; nobody I knew

had ever been to university, not one person.

I can remember the money side of it: getting a grant of £100 a term, something like that, and my mum and dad sending me £16 a month, which paid for the rent. Sixteen pounds a month! I can remember going to the bank and getting £5 out, and it'd last you the week.

I came from a pit village in the north-east, a Category D village, which meant it was dead because no more mining could take place, so the people around me were unemployed. I studied Law at university, and nearly all my fellow students had parents who were high up in the law, and their lives were totally different. I felt very self-conscious about being the underdog. All the people from state schools did – not academically, but socially.

People were still very stuck-up about going to university in the seventies. I remember a friend of mine saying to me, Do you realize that we are the top 10 per cent of society? Now, 50 per cent go, and they're all doing better than me.

I was the first one in my family to go to college. We didn't know what it entailed, how to do it, how to get a grant, how to apply. It was a whole new ball game for the whole family. Moving away from home at the age of eighteen was very unusual; my father was part of a very big family, one of eleven children who all lived round and about. Knowing how to manage on your own was hard, because I was used to having people up the road, round the corner. Managing on a grant was a strange event.

When I went to college, we went through the whole thing of buying a trunk. We had to go to the Co-op because my mum wanted the stamps. I packed this trunk assiduously, then my dad drove me to the nearest big station and left me. I came back home from college at Christmas and my dad asked me where I'd been. He was such a self-centred man. He'd noticed I'd gone, but he had no notion of where I was.

I left school in 1978, when I was eighteen. I went to secretarial college for a year and thoroughly enjoyed that, it seemed much more grown-up, going to Leeds on the train every day. They were very strict, and pushed you through everything. We did exams straight away so we were achieving, and that appealed to me. I liked the efficiency of it. It was the complete opposite of everything I'd learnt at school – or not learnt.

At the end of my first degree I knew that an Oxbridge education in Britain was no longer enough to get you a job and a career for life, so I went off and did a Management degree for a year.

The college I was at in the early seventies was single-sex. By the end of the seventies, the Jesus College rugby team had sunk to unprecedented lows because it no longer had this solid intake of Welsh rugby-playing boys; instead, the tutors had chosen the much more hard-working and reliable women.

I did too much work at college, and not enough wider-scale things; there were lots of things I didn't know about that some people were ticking off as part of their relentless route, via secretaryship of the Union and membership of the Conservative Association, to the City, where they became things like commodity brokers and were assured of instant wealth. So there was this divide, because most of us went on to become teachers.

I can remember sleeping an enormous amount my first term at East Anglia, because I was rather shocked by the whole event. For the first year we had rooms in converted Nissen huts, six miles from the campus. We cycled to the campus, which had been built on an old golf course near Norwich, so there was a fair amount of antagonism towards us. The University of East Anglia in those days attracted a lot of Sloaney characters. History of Art was a popular course, with rather elegant young women and debauched young men.

I scraped into Keele University in 1975. I had a great time there, really enjoyed it. Then I started all over again and went to Sussex, I managed to wangle an extra grant.
I found Sussex better academically. I arrived at a time when the hippie thing was at an end, punk had come in, Brighton was pretty shabby and run down and the university was not a very popular place. At weekends the campus virtually emptied and people went off to London. Brighton wasn't the buzzing and exciting place it is now by any means.

I applied late to do a Business Studies degree at Southbank University – and it was probably the smartest thing I ever did. Business Studies was in its infancy then, there were very few colleges that did it. That degree was the big thing in my life in the early seventies. We did what was called a thick sandwich course: two years at college, a year at work, and a year back at college. A thin sandwich was two years, six months and six months.

The seventies was really a split decade for me, the first half was all college and that sort of thing. The last year of college I was probably the richest student you've ever met, because Gulf Oil sponsored me. They paid me £1,000, plus salary for a month at Christmas and Easter, plus a grant of £500 towards my thesis, which I did on the energy business. I was rich compared with other students, and it was great. I had a terrific time.

First jobs

I worked in an advertising agency, I got £3,000 a year. I shared a house in Putney with these incredibly right-wing guys; one of them was in the SAS. So when I became a punk they kicked me out. They liked having a punk at the advertising agency, it gave them a bit of cachet.

By the end of the seventies I was working at *Time Out*, which was like being at the centre of the universe. It was tremendously exciting – the best of times. It's where I got my education, my ideas, my passion for the underdog and my absolute loathing for the ruling class.

I remember using one of the very first word processors, when a floppy disk really was a floppy disk. That was in about 1979, and it was amazing what you could do with it, you know, delete a word, paste a paragraph. So technology was beginning to come through, but it was still jolly expensive.

A lot of the people I was at school or university with went to work in the City. And the money was crap, then. The starting salary in 1979 for a big merchant bank would have been about £6,000 a year. I remember Goldman Sachs coming along and offering £12,000 a year, way above anything anyone else was offering, so I applied to them.

In the mid-seventies I was a temp, which was great. There was lots of work. Working wasn't what you aspired to do, it was what you did because you'd run out of money. As a secretary it was great; you could beam in for a couple of days then call in sick. I was terrible. I cheated my employers terribly when I think about it. I didn't really know what business was all about, and I didn't really care. I wanted to experiment with everything, and work was too straight.

When I left school in 1976 I spent two years working in a pie and mash shop, getting paid under the counter. I was paid a fortune at the time; I was on about £200 a week, tax-free. And I just pissed it up the wall.

I started my first job in 1970. It was a small, avant-garde publishing company and the office was at the top of several flights of rickety stairs in Soho. I ran the switchboard, typed the contracts (with carbon paper, still) and manned the reception desk. I got £15 a week, and no one bothered about tax. If we wanted something copied we had to go down the road to a photocopying bureau – no small office then had such a high-tech piece of equipment as a photocopying machine. It seems extraordinary now, but it wasn't so long ago.

I got a very lucrative job selling make-up on a party plan basis, called Miss Mary of Sweden, when I was sixteen or seventeen. You bought your kit, and you set up the parties, and you got 27 per cent commission on everything you sold. I had my little Mini, and I did two parties a week, and I made quite a lot of money.

My first job paid £5,500, in 1979, a Scale 1 teaching post. I thought it was all right. We bought our first house then for £12,500 and I remember thinking, my god, we'll never pay this mortgage off.

I was determined to become a filmmaker, and I did every dirty job going. I lived in garrets and worked my way up until at the end of the seventies I was accepted by the BBC on one of their training schemes. That began a rich chapter in my life.

In the seventies, I was quite concerned to get myself into a comfortable hole, at least somewhere where I was intellectually stimulated, which is why I switched from management to the Bar. The most modern piece of equipment I ever saw at the Bar was a dictaphone. The rest was scratching with quill pens, essentially doing something that might have happened two hundred years earlier. Waistcoats, separate collars, the wig and all that. You needed a considerable outlay just to dress. So there were people of very great ability who were simply financially broken at the Bar, and couldn't ever become barristers. They either changed to become solicitors – and there was a tremendous snobbery at the Bar – or they simply left and did other things, and they were some of the brightest and the best.

I went to work for Gulf Oil in the time of the big oil crisis, in 1974. Oil prices went up by 300 per cent overnight. They said to me, You're going to have to work on this oil industry emergency committee, which was at the time responsible for all the oil being imported and exported from the UK. I mean, I was thrown into this meeting with people who'd been working in the industry for twenty years, and I was a trainee.

I had one good friend who joined the army to get out of the only job he could find, moving furniture. He had no qualifications; there was nothing else he could do.

I moved down to London from the north-east and my first job was working as a temp at Cunard. Their offices were luxurious, and I was gobsmacked at the amount people paid for their holidays on the QEII.

Somewhere to live

I had terrible problems finding a place to live in London. It was desperate, just terrible, trying to get a flat in those days. It's what plagued me all through my life in London. I lived in seventeen different places, and if I'd found somewhere nice my life might have been very different.

In the early seventies a group of eight of us shared a huge house in Ealing for two years. It wasn't a squat, it was a rather grand old Victorian house with seven bedrooms and two

bathrooms and a lovely old garden full of pear trees and Virginia creeper. We paid £40 a week in rent. But we treated it really badly. One night in the living room one guy, looking down at his now-cold cup of tea, decided to chuck the remains against the wall. That became the Weeping Wall. We chucked everything at it: wine, beer, tea, whatever. It was great fun, but really disgusting.

I remember sharing ghastly houses in Liverpool around Sefton Park in the mid to late seventies, putting up with the damp and putting the money in the meter. We didn't have central heating in those houses, of course. I got into a hall of residence in 1978 and that was my first experience of central heating. Magic.

One of the ways to find accommodation in London if you didn't have much money in those days was to register with the GLC for one of what was known as their 'hard to rent' flats. These were places where ordinary families wouldn't live, on estates with high crime rates. I lived on one estate like that in Tulse Hill, south of Brixton, and it was quite a tough place. I was burgled as I was moving in. People tried to break in all the time.

They did a refurbishment campaign on my estate. They'd refurbish a flat. They'd fit central heating, gas fires, then that night the tinkers and others on the estate would come and carry the kitchen units, fires, et cetera away. I remember hearing a terrible banging one night, and going up to have a look. And the people a few floors above had been cut off, presumably for non-payment of gas bills, so they were improvising gas piping from a nearby flat. They were hammering the tubes together.

I'd never lived before alongside people who didn't use bins or bin liners. They'd just throw it all out the window. There'd be food, food wrappings, furniture, coming down your block of flats to smash on the pavement outside.

Squats

The first squat I lived in was horrible. All the squats I lived in were horrible, really. The Greater London Council used to buy up all these houses, streets of them, when they were empty and in bad condition. They'd put corrugated iron all around them, then they'd go in and smash up all the lavatories and basins, all the plumbing, so we couldn't use them. The idea was that one day the council would renovate these areas and make money out of real estate, but they never did. They just bought up streets and streets of houses all over London and boarded them up, smashed them up so that people couldn't squat in them. But we were all homeless, so we did squat in them.

I knew people who lived in squats who draped the whole place in muslin, things like that, keeping the nasty stuff out. One lot managed to squat in a row of five houses with a communal garden out the back, and they had the most amazing parties.

Our squat was in a row of corrugated iron, with a few houses in between. It was a two-up, two-down off the Caledonian Road. And there we'd all sit. Most people didn't go to work, most people didn't even bother to get dressed, as I recall. We basically floated around in pretty blankets, and sat on the floor against the wall, on cushions because there was virtually no furniture, and smoked dope. And everybody waited while somebody went out to score every night. Nobody spoke, because we were all too stoned and it wasn't cool to speak. I found that very stressful. It used to really annoy me. I was very chatty, but there was one guy called Roger who literally didn't speak for years. It was unbelievable.

I went out to work, so I put on all this gear to go to work. But when I came back in the evenings I used to change in front of the mirror in the telephone kiosk outside the tube station – like Superman in reverse. I'd put on all my hippie gear and take all my make-up off, because no one in the squat wore make-up, it wasn't cool.

We didn't eat much. There was no take-away except for fish and chips in those days, and none of us cooked. I remember the cats eating, but I don't remember us eating.

There was some recognition that the housing situation was appalling, because the squatter's rules were that if you got into a squat and nobody evicted you in the first twenty-four hours, you could actually change the locks and you were then legal.

We were served notice by the council to vacate our first squat and needed another one in a hurry, so I found one. It was a really grand place, very smart nowadays. It looked empty, and big, so we got in there, stayed twenty-four hours, changed the locks and Bob's your uncle. It was freezing, this house, because it was really big. It was mid-winter, and one night we were all sitting around the big fireplace (the heat source was absolutely central to everything; you'd all sit around in a semicircle) in our grandmas' fur coats. And one of the guys came in, and trailing

behind him was this very upright suit. He said, Good evening, and the guy who brought him in said, This is the owner. The owner then explained that, actually, this house was owned by him, not the council. He was selling it to them in a couple of weeks, but he had to sell it with vacant possession. So would we mind terribly, just for the days they were exchanging contracts, moving out, then we could move back in again? So that's what we did.

We were freezing all the time. That's what I remember more than anything. Also, not having any plumbing was pretty rough. We didn't wash very much, it's true. We used buckets, or sometimes there'd be a basin on the landing that hadn't been smashed. It was pretty horrible.

A lot of the people in the squats were completely out of their trees a lot of the time, and some very violent things happened. I was really scared at night. Then I met some normal people and discovered feminism, and left the squats behind.

FRANCIS WHEEN
Columnist on the *Guardian*, a performer on the *News Quiz*, a man about *Private Eye* and the author of a highly acclaimed biography of Karl Marx.

Too young for the 60s and too old for punk, I had to make do with the early 70s – that grim era of Mud, Sweet and the three-day-week. In 1973, aged sixteen, I wrote to Charles Shaar Murray, a former contributor to the *Schoolkids' Oz* who was now one of the stars of *New Musical Express*, to ask if I should 'drop out'. I interpreted his silence as tacit approval. A few weeks later I slung my guitar on my back, donned a beret from the Harrow School cadet force (which, I hoped, would give me the air of a young Che Guevara) and ran away to London.

My destination was the BIT Alternative Help and Information Centre in Westbourne Park, a kind of hippie Citizens' Advice Bureau about which I had read in the underground press. 'I've come to join the alternative society, man,' I declared. There were weary groans. 'You're too late,' someone muttered.

After a couple of weeks in a squat round the corner I began to see his point. My youthful enthusiasm ('Let's build the counter-culture right here!') was not shared by the other residents, who preferred to spend the days smoking themselves into a stupor while reading – or, worse still, writing – dreary science-fiction epics. To shut me up, however, they eventually agreed to try out my plan for self-sufficiency. Every night for a week we broke into derelict buildings, stripping out the copper wire and piping. When the pile of swag filled most of our main room, we summoned the local scrap metal dealer – who offered us a quid for the lot.

'Now do you see?' one of my fellow-squatters demanded triumphantly. 'You can get more than that by just signing on the dole – and you don't have to risk a broken leg by climbing into some dark empty house with no floorboards.' Fed up with their lassitude and defeatism, I rang my mother and announced that I was dropping back in.

I don't know where my old housemates are now. Still 'getting their heads together'? Or standing for Parliament on behalf of the New Labour party and furiously denying that they ever inhaled? But I do know what became of my hippie hero Charles Shaar Murray, whom I met for the first time just the other day. He's writing a regular column for ... the *Daily Telegraph*.

I went back to living in a squat after breaking up with my boyfriend, and I started a relationship with someone who turned out to be the Casanova of Clapham. He slept with everybody, and he supplied everybody with dope. This was a very big community of squatters, in Rectory Gardens. We all drank in the same pubs and we all slept with each other.

One day, three guys walked down the middle of the street, one with an iron bar and one swinging a great big chain. Everybody came out of their houses, and there was a street battle. People stopped at the end of the street with babies in prams and watched what was going on. These guys were on a different trip, they were on speed, they were red-eyed and really scary.

A lot of people in the squats did fall by the wayside in one form or another. A lot of women fell by the wayside in order to stay close to their men. The men later went into smack, and it was just awful.

Food

In the early seventies my boyfriend and I would eat out once a week, at a café in Soho. It used to cost us about £2. It was one step up from a greasy spoon – but a very shallow step.

It was a big treat to go out to Kentucky Fried Chicken. And once a week we'd go out to a Wimpy Bar. It was considered quite upmarket.

We used to cook those Vesta meals a lot.

Horrible dried curries that you put water in. Chicken Supreme, too. And Chow Mein, with the crispy noodles you put on top. That was considered fairly cosmopolitan.

We'd go out to the occasional Indian restaurant, on birthdays, occasions like that. There was a restaurant in Manchester called El Greco's, which doesn't exist any more, and it was a bring-your-own-wine Greek place with long tables, dirt cheap.

We didn't go out to eat much because where was there to go?

North-eastern food in the seventies consisted of a wholesome breakfast, dinner if you were at home at twelve o'clock, tea at four o'clock. Dinner was always a proper meal; tea was always bread, cakes, scones, biscuits and a cup of tea.

In our shared house, we'd all have a game of darts while we were cooking, then we'd all eat together. It went on for a couple of hours, it was a really good social thing.

I was invited to my boyfriend's flat for a meal of spaghetti bolognese. Well, we didn't have that in the north-east; where had this come from?

My parents, at the beginning of the seventies, were into meat and two veg every night. And then they started getting into spaghetti bolognese, which was very chic, very sophisticated. And then my dad would get even braver and do a curry. Towards the end of the decade, we would sit around at six o'clock on a Saturday night watching *The Generation Game* and eating pizza. We thought we were the height of chic.

It was always, go round to the offie and get a bottle of Pomagne because *The Fugitive* was on. And get a packet of salt and vinegar crisps while you're at it, or an Aero.

My mother bought a packet of Vesta curry round about 1972, and I came in from playing football outside and said, What's that smell? She said, That's your dinner, we're going to have curry. I said, Oh, I don't think I'll like that. My mother and brother said, Try it, go on. So we ate it, and I liked it and they didn't.

A meal always had to have potatoes, whether it was chipped or boiled or whatever. The staple diet has changed now, but then we never had pasta or rice at home. Every meal came with potatoes. But that decade was the start of the change.

Shepherd's pie seemed to occur a lot.

I remember in 1976 a friend coming over from America and being aghast because she bought a can of Coke that wasn't chilled. It never occurred to us to put things like Coke in the fridge.

Did you ever see *The Young Ones*? That could have been me in the seventies. I once had a celebration meal to finish off the autumn term before going home for Christmas, and we cooked steak and mushrooms, a massive meal for lots of people. Then, I suppose because we were male, we left the washing up, and we came back to it after Christmas. It was just one huge mound of mould ...

Steaks with prawns on the top, called Surf 'n' Turf. And prawn cocktails. Very seventies. And Black Forest gateau seemed to be the exotic pudding.

We ate a lot of instant food. Vesta beef curries were brilliant.

I remember making a curry once out of lumps of cheese and a curry sauce. The cheese was supposed to melt.

I can remember going to restaurants for the first time. Italian seemed to be the thing. But curry became popular, especially after six pints of lager.

Macro rules OK

Do you remember macrobiotic food? The purists had a ball with that one, didn't they?

Fad diets really got going in the seventies. A friend told me that his girlfriend had gone on a purge, eating nothing but fruit for a fortnight to rid her body of toxins. I'd never heard anything so ridiculous.

It was an experimental time. It was something I went on to base almost the rest of my life on: the change from being a meat-

London's complete natural food centre featuring a full range of organically grown vegetables and grains.

Price lists not sent.

10.00 to 6.00 Mon-Sat
6.30 Friday.

CERES 269a Portobello Rd   229·5571

NOT JUST A LOAD OF OLD LENTILS
ROSE ELLIOT

eater to eating healthy foods, whole foods, becoming a vegetarian.

Vegetarian food became really big: Rose Elliot's books, Cranks restaurant in London. Henderson's restaurant in Edinburgh was a revelation: fabulous vegetarian food. My mother was very into all that so I was subjected to a lot of lentil roasts. She made yoghurt, she made all our bread.

Parents of a friend of mine were very much into *The Good Life*, living on a farm outside Ripon with hens and goats. It was the first time I ever had yoghurt. I saw it on the breakfast table and said, What's this?

There was a health food shop called On the Eighth Day, where we started buying the oat flakes, the bran flakes and whatever to make our own muesli. I remember reading articles in the Sunday papers about health, and starting to think about healthy eating, starting to change the diet. That was a big change. Gone was the Sunday roast.

There were strange people in my block of flats, pre-punks or Goths or something, whose faces were flour-white and who only wore black and whose hair was black, and they were my idea of vegetarians.

Household style

Everything in the seventies seemed to be brown. Everyone went crazy with brown wallpaper, brown carpets, brown furniture. Shagpile carpets – they go with brown wallpaper.

We were the first family I knew to have continental quilts. We had dark brown nylon sheets, and dark brown towels. That was really groovy.

We had lots of Habitat furniture, very Scandinavian. Bright orange seats and very pale wood, it was radical. And Danish-style cutlery.

I had a Biba baked bean tin; I wish I'd kept it. I bought it at the big department store in the old Derry and Tom's building.

We painted all the walls of our flat purple, and had pink and blue light bulbs. We used to grope our way around.

Do you remember the electricity meters you had to feed with shillings? They were so frustrating: a) if you didn't have any change, and b) if the landlord hadn't emptied them. You couldn't put any more money in if they hadn't been emptied, so you had no electricity even if you had the money. It was hideous.

I was really into macramé. I'd make macramé plant holders, macramé wall hangings, you name it. I thought it was the most wonderful thing, really earthy and natural.

I was so proud of the brown velvet sofa I bought in 1979. It was the first major piece of furniture I'd ever bought. I made all my friends come and admire it.

I bought my first stereo system in 1970 for about £50. It was wonderful, having speakers instead of a little record player. I'd buy an LP every week.

Hi-fis were very important then, you'd go into someone's place and check out their hi-fi system and judge them for it.

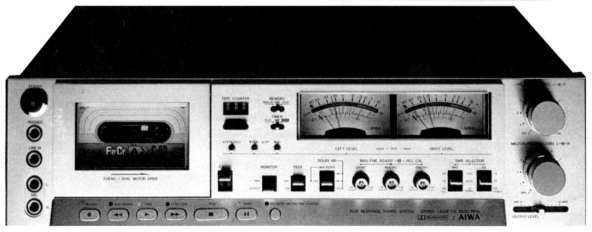

My brother and I had a beanbag each. I was passionately into Mary Quant, and I had the daisy print on purple on my curtains, on my duvet cover (duvets had just come in, and we all got duvets), on pillowcases, and even a Mary Quant silver pin cushion, covered in the daisy fabric, which I still have.

My parents bought this super-duper new house on this new housing estate; it was deemed very posh. You were moving away from the thirties' semis into the seventies' detached houses.

I remember my mum and dad kitting out their semi with all this G-Plan furniture. That was really a big thing. If you had G-Plan, you were it, you were someone. It was teak, boxy, and there was a round table with glass in the middle.

I come from a very working-class background, and this was a time when that particular segment of society was changing more than any other. We found gadgets for the first time. We didn't know how to use them, but we could get them. Things like coffee percolators: we didn't know what to put in, or how much, so we had dreadful coffee. But we'd seen them on TV and in the magazines, and a whole new avenue of life was opening up before us.

The onslaught of materialism, of consumerism, began in the seventies. I remember my dad putting a central heating system into our thirties' semi. In these semis, it was all the rage to knock through a hole between the front room and the dining room and put in these pebbled-glass doors.

I remember lots of lime green and orange. And swirly carpets and swirly tiles. And hessian.

My father was a chief superintendent of police, but in the early seventies we lived in a house that had one bathroom for the five of us; I slept in a boxroom that was literally six foot by five foot. When I look back, we were poverty-stricken. We didn't have central heating. I used to get condensation inside my window that used to freeze. That was the way houses were, then.

Sex ... for girls

It was pretty disastrous for young women in the seventies. The sixties had opened this Pandora's box. We did have widely available contraception, and I went on the Pill, but I felt constantly under really bad pressure.

The thing coming out of the sixties was this crap about the sexual revolution and free love, but actually what you became terribly aware of in the seventies was that it wasn't free for women, it was an absolute imposition. The Pill removed your autonomy. Suddenly, you were supposed to think that it was absolutely fabulous to wave your legs in the air and get fucked. And it didn't mean that the blokes knew anything better; they would still have been better off stirring tea with their willies. And what did women get out of it? Lots of bad sex that they probably didn't want, men thinking that this was Christmas, and lots of sexually transmitted diseases.

I went to live in a huge house in Shepherd's Bush that had sixteen Aussies living in it. It had four floors, plus basement, and it was really rough. I had to get a lock put on my bedroom door, the guys were all such animals.

The Pill was available from the beginning. I seem to have been on the Pill all my life – after trying a few alternatives like diaphragms, which were absolute agony, and coils. You'd hear all these stories of coils being fished out of people's stomachs, remember them?

My mother got a twin-tub washing machine, which was supposed to be a great labour saver, but she still had to slave over it every Saturday, transferring water from one tub to another. It didn't help her life in any way whatsoever.

We moved in 1970 into a brand-new house, so everything was very modern. The kitchen was all flowers, and there was a lot of orange and purple, big patterns and big stripes.

Sexual relations at that time were really tough for women. Boys enjoyed it because we were all on the Pill, and the line was, we're all friends, we all sleep with each other, and it's all fine. Actually, it never was fine for us girls. But you had to pretend that it was. I mean, we weren't just promiscuous slags, it was part of being a hippie. We believed in free love. But it was so painful.

I felt no pressure to have sex before I was ready. I felt pretty much in control of all that. I made sure, at the ripe old age of sixteen, when the dreaded deed was done, that I was on the Pill first.

It wasn't like those days in the fifties or even the early sixties when they'd call you a slag, or 'loose'. By the seventies, it was considered really uncool to still be a virgin when you were eighteen.

There was lots of sex, but no intercourse – which was great fun, when you look back on it. I was as avid for it as anyone, and there was lots of exploratory goings-on, but I was very aware that there was no way I was going to get pregnant. I hadn't talked about it with my mother, it was just an awareness I had.

My boyfriend and I were literally about to get married before my mother would allow us to share a room in her house. We'd lived together for years, but when we went to stay with my parents she'd say, Not in my house. It seems unbelievable now.

Oddly enough, it was my dad who told me to get on the Pill. He said, Best thing that bloody happened to your mother. That sorted her out. Soon as you can, get on it!

Sexually transmitted diseases didn't feature large in my life. I thought, Now I'm on the Pill, if I want to go to bed with that bloke, I could make a play for him and do it, and there'd be no comeback. It was my choice, and my decision. My life. So I guess that in

some ways that led to, not laddish but lassish behaviour among certain groups. Finally there were gangs of eighteen-year-old women going for lads we fancied, downing pints and cornering them and making a play, and taking them back to our scruffy little damp-riddled house in Liverpool.

I had pressure from my first boyfriend to have sex, but I kept saying no because I was only fifteen. My parents were a big influence. I worried about what they'd think. We had a great time and experimented a lot, and felt a lot for each other, but we didn't actually go the whole way. But not for the want of him trying.

My friend Sarah had a boyfriend. And the whole topic of the day was whether you had french-kissed or not, how you did it, and what it was like. And Sarah, bless her cotton socks, showed me. I can't look at her lips today without remembering …

If you had sex with someone you were a real slapper. In the sixth form I was chairman of the Virgins' Society. I don't know how it started, but it was very serious. We all honestly believed that if you lost your virginity before your A-levels, you would fail. I finally lost mine the day before my German A-level. I went to the Family Planning Clinic, I had to go through all this trauma, and I remember him sitting on the wall outside while I got all these pills. And I only got a D.

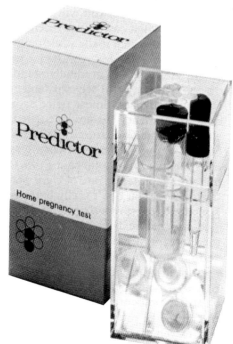

... and for boys

It was a fairly easy decade for us blokes. Most girls were on the Pill. I don't know what the sixties were like, but in the seventies sex was there and relatively widespread, and safe. It was probably the last decade when sex was safe. I mean you had to worry about getting someone pregnant, or getting a dose or something like that, but it wouldn't kill you. You could have sex and rest easy. No one had even heard of AIDS. If you got a dose, you'd just nip down the clinic and stay off the booze for a month. You're done. You're back in the saddle. Once you got into the eighties, you'd think twice before whipping it out.

All we used to do was walk around the streets trying to chat girls up at weekends. My one aim in life was to have a girlfriend. Skinny boys with no bums, walking around in our flares.

We went hitchhiking around Scotland in the summer of 1975, and I had to buy a wedding ring at Woolworth's to get into a cottage. Then my girlfriend had to remember to put it on.

You didn't have gay people in the seventies, you had poofs, especially if you came from a mining community. It was us and them.

Intellectually, my school created the groundwork. The plays and literature that I was reading, such as Orton, with issues such as homosexuality, the plays by Wesker and Osborne; film and theatre had begun to create an idea in my mind. I had the idea that women were just like ice creams: you met them, slept with them, and went on. I thought everyone did that all the time, devoid of feelings or relationships. The James Bond model.

Abortions

Getting your arse out there to march, getting two hundred thousand women together meant that you could get an abortion, whereas at the beginning of the seventies, getting an abortion was terrifying. It was dangerous, it cost a lot of money, it was absolute sleazy backstreet stuff, you had no idea if you were going to be OK or not. The danger of abortion in the early seventies was probably the same as it had been in the thirties; by the end of the decade, having an abortion was possible, safe and affordable, and you didn't have to sneak around in the dead of the night feeling like – and being – a criminal.

In 1970 having an abortion was life-threatening and terrifying, and by 1978 it was not. And your peers were out there marching shoulder to shoulder supporting your right, women's right, to choose. Making it possible to feel safe, and that it didn't matter if you were poor. Whereas in 1971, having to find £250 to have an abortion was terrifying, absolutely terrifying.

Marriage, seventies style

In 1970, people were still forced into shotgun weddings. But by 1979, they'd gone. These days, I doubt whether any young people know what a shotgun wedding is.

I met a girl when I was fifteen, in 1974, got engaged to her when I was seventeen, married her when I was twenty. Childhood sweetheart thing. But then I started working on this newspaper, where I met all these different people. Middle-class people. And this whole new world opened up to me, but my girlfriend had left school at age sixteen and was a secretary. So we got married because it was the done thing, but it lasted three months.

VALERIE GROVE

A journalist since 1968 when she started on the *Evening Standard*. Since written – mostly interviews — for the *Sunday Times* and *The Times*. Author of two biographies, of the authors Dodie Smith and Laurie Lee.

Ours was a very mid-1970s wedding. The colours that year were brown and cream. The bride and groom each wore cream suits; the groom's trousers were the last word in flares. Even the invitations had to be brown ink on cream card. My previous wedding had been a thoroughly 1960s one – everyone in mini-skirts, in Hampstead registry office. But my new husband insisted on the whole traditional C of E deal, at his favourite Wren church, St Vedast, near St Paul's. Its Rector was too high-minded ("I hate divorce") to marry us, but let us have the church, so we had to find a priest who would bless us there. The Revd Chad Varah, founder of the Samaritans, obliged, with "statements of commitment" to replace the marriage vows.

But first, we had one of the last civil weddings at the ancient Guildhall in the City of London. Then there was the wedding lunch at the house of a friend in Islington: a long table for 22 in a room leading into a walled garden. Then to St Vedast for the blessing, with me now in cream lace, the most expensive dress I'd ever worn (£46).

Finally, to the reception – which stamped it indelibly as a 1975 occasion because it was the last wedding reception ever held at Biba's Roof Garden in Kensington High Street. When we'd discussed the catering (kir and canapés) with Barbara Hulanicki's husband, Stephen Fitz-Simon, he confided that Biba would be closing its doors forever that summer. It was the end of a brief, heady era: Biba's keynote cream fringed sun-shades were still on the terrace, the gardens were still the glorious old Derry & Tom's garden, the women wore long floating Biba dresses, and the men favoured cream suits. It was the last day of the early summer heatwave of that year. The cake was made by the young woman who wrote the *Evening Standard* cookery column – Delia Smith. And after the speeches and the poem we recited (about our courtship, as colleagues on the *Standard*: "We dined on a boat/And that evening afloat/Spliced our byline together forever") there was dancing to a Spanish guitar.

As we left for our honeymoon the heatwave ended, the heavens opened – and we'd got a parking ticket in Derry Street. But the traffic warden got the registration number wrong, so we never got the fine. A lucky omen.

When I got my first job in 1977 and became pregnant immediately, I conned my employers – the Law Society – into giving me four months off sick, because there were no maternity provisions then, no one had even thought of it before.

At the end of the seventies we were expecting a child, I had a job, my husband was a student doing post-grad social work, and the attitudes we were met with were interesting. He was in a placement, and the message he was given strongly was that if he took any time off, even for the birth, it was going to be frowned upon. I had very nice but very paternalistic employers who tried their best to bend the rules to help.

I got married at Burnt Oak Registry Office in June 1970 wearing a purple satin Biba nightdress and an antique grey silk tablecloth worn as a shawl, which had a lovely long fringe on it. Opposite the registry office was the local Woolworth's, with the graffiti 'Burnt Oak Boot Boys' scrawled across the wall.

We went to a registry office, the only people there apart from us were our parents, and that was perfectly OK by us. A strand of working-class culture is to spend your life savings on a big traditional wedding. I can still remember my sister's wedding, all that stupid stuff. We didn't want any of that.

In the late seventies, we lived in Warrington and some women there only read the paper after their husband had looked through it and marked which bits they could read. In some families, the guy would get home from work before the woman and he'd sit in the bloody chair and wait, he wouldn't even make a cup of tea.

Drink ...
We used to go to a music venue at Camden Town, and they had cheap drinks before 10 p.m. So we'd get there at ten to ten and order three thousand Tequila Sunrises and sit there at these little round tables completely covered in drinks, nowhere to put your cigarettes down even.

There was a council estate where my friends and I used to hang out, with an underground car park in the middle. There weren't that many places to go when you're thirteen or fourteen. So we used to go to an off-licence and buy a litre of cider and a packet of Polos. Then we'd go two or three floors down, where it was all rusted cars and water. And we'd drink these litre bottles of cider. I remember being pissed as a fart, wandering over London Fields, looking at the stars, falling flat on my back, whole world going round and round, then jumping on the 253 back to Bethnal Green, eating Polos all the way so that my mother wouldn't smell the beer on me. Staggering in the front door, going straight to bed. It was only recently that my mum said to me, Who do you think you were kidding? Staggering in, stinking of Polos and cider ... And I'd thought I'd been so clever.

I started drinking at pubs when I was thirteen. I used to hang around Hackney and Bethnal Green. Friday, Saturday, Sunday nights, all spent at the pub. I remember standing in a pub when I was about fifteen, talking to the owner, and he said, I got raided last night. There's so many youngsters in the pubs these days, you don't know how old they are, do you?

My dad made home-brewed lager for many years and he let me have some in a sherry glass at my sister's New Year's Eve engagement party. While no one was looking I had several refills and I was violently sick. Mam emptied the rest of the barrel down the sink. Dad was furious.

Being a teenager, you're allowed a passing-out phase, aren't you?

In the early seventies we'd go to Eel Pie Island, and to the Strand on the Green at Kew. Hanging out in these really nice pubs. We drove there and back, because no one gave a thought to drinking and driving.

We did a huge amount of drinking in the seventies. I remember being often drunk at work. In 1977, which was of course the Jubilee year, Princess

Margaret came to the performance of the pageant at my school. We had all our instructions for the visit. We had to put a bottle of Gordon's gin in the ladies' toilet.

One of my housemates in college lived in Blackpool, and five of us went there for the weekend, to stay at this lad's mum's house. We were all very polite and well-behaved, as you'd expect. Then we went to the Bierkeller one night and had massive steins of lager. We were drunk, but drunk laughing as opposed to drunk falling over, we were having a good time. It was

about two o'clock in the morning, we were walking back to my friend's house, and we passed this cinema with *Saturday Night Fever* on the front in great big letters. So we got up on each other's shoulders and took the *Sa* and the *ay* from the letters, and turned it into *turd Night Fever*. It was so funny, it was ridiculous but hilarious. Then we very carefully put the letters in a corner by the door, so the cinema people would be able to put them back up, and carried on down the road. Two or three streets on, a Black Maria stopped by us, three big bobbies got out and said, We're going to arrest you for the vandalism at the pictures. To which we replied, Give over. We all laughed. We didn't think we'd done anything wrong; nothing was broken. But they took us to the central police station and put us all into one cell. Then the arresting officer came over and said, Who actually took the letters off? And one of us said, I did it, let these other lads off, I'll pay for it. So they took him outside the cells and beat him up – we were all watching through these little spy holes. I called out to this policeman, I've got your number! I'll report you! They were quite concerned, because there were now four witnesses who were quite sober and very angry, and obviously quite articulate. A police inspector came in the early morning and said, If you stop all the accusations about being beaten up, we'll stop the prosecution. So we all left, but I was absolutely outraged.

When we went to parties we'd take Babycham

Heineken refreshes the parts other beers cannot reach.

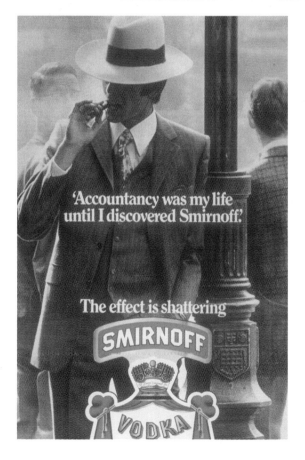

'Accountancy was my life until I discovered Smirnoff.'

The effect is shattering

SMIRNOFF VODKA

or cider. Then people would get drunk and it became a big issue. They'd fall over and be ill, and I hated all of that, the trauma that it caused.

My first boyfriend took me to this terrible pub in Maidstone, by the prison. I was fourteen and I'd never been into a pub before. He said, What are you having to drink? I hadn't a clue. So I said, A dry martini and lemonade, because that was what my mother drank and I didn't know of any other drinks. I didn't know it was illegal to drink alcohol if you weren't eighteen, I was that innocent.

I can remember when girls couldn't go into pubs on their own. No way; you just couldn't.

I'd spent a lot of time in the West End in the sixties when I was a kid, I grew up there. But it changed. By the time the seventies came around, the West End scene had got a lot harder. You had to be pretty careful. A lot of the clubs, for instance, had got a drink licence, which they didn't have in the sixties. And they got really tough about letting people in, and they got more expensive.

... and drugs

I did a lot of speed, little blue pills, blues, in the seventies. We'd stay up all night. Pot was around, but I'd been to Morocco with my sister and had far too much marijuana, which luckily put me off for life.

The only drug I touched was marijuana, and I didn't like it. I did start smoking cigarettes in the seventies. Everybody smoked, so you just did.

Camberwell was really rough; coming back from the tube late at night was really scary. I lived in a flat in an area around the back of some factories. One night we got broken into, a stone came through the front bedroom window, and the cops came round. I remember looking at this chest in front of the window, with a plant on top of it. And all three of us suddenly remembered what this plant was as we stood there with the policeman looking at the hole in the window.

The big drama of the evening in our flat was who was going out to score, and who wasn't, and when they were coming back. We used to go around the carpet very carefully, because you hoped there might be a lump of dope.

My friend Dave went to live in a flat on Baker Street, and he set up this enormously elaborate hydroponic system on the roof for growing dope. But he was training to be a doctor, and was just about to qualify when somebody grassed on him, and he was nicked.

My brother put some dope into the spaghetti our mother prepared for us one night. It goes straight to your stomach. She woke us up in the middle of the night wanting to call a doctor, and we sat up all night long, trying to persuade her not to call a doctor. We had several sessions when we got stoned with Mum. She always got the worst effects: 'Ooh, I feel dizzy … ooh, I've got a terrible headache … ooh, I don't feel right.' Mostly, I couldn't stop laughing.

Of course, we thought dope ought to be legalized.

Some of my friends took a bit of speed, but I never really did. If I combine dope with alcohol, I feel sick. So I had to make the choice, drugs or alcohol. No contest.

We moved down to London in early 1970, and tried to join the drug scene there. We found it much more paranoid than in the north. People were very wary, and didn't like us approaching them at all. We began to feel paranoid ourselves.

The first time I was ever passed a chillum, I pretended I knew all about how to smoke it. But I didn't have a clue. I held it like you hold a joint, and everything began to fall out the end. I was so embarrassed.

We took a lot of acid in the early seventies, and spent a lot of time feeling paranoid in pubs in Ealing. Sitting there feeling that everyone knew, and everyone was staring and pointing and whispering. It was much better to stay home and palpitate there.

Ripon had a teacher training college, so there were lots of student teachers around. It had quite a vibrant student union, and we'd all go up there for the discos. It was great. There were subsidized drinks, and every weekend there'd be something organized by the college. Lots of interesting people, too. It was the first time I'd been exposed to dope, through all these embryonic infant-school teachers. I thought they were so bohemian. They had parties and wore cheesecloth and patchouli oil. The smell of patchouli oil still takes me straight back to that time.

I took my first LSD trip around 1972, when I was sixteen, and I'd been thrown out of my boarding school for drinking when I was thirteen, so I was a bit of a tearaway really.

There was cocaine around towards the end of the seventies – at least, I heard about it, but I never had the opportunity to try it. There were lots of amphetamines around, a leftover from the sixties.

There was quite a widespread heroin problem. My brother died of a heroin overdose when he was twenty-one, in 1969, and my mother started a charity in London called the APA, the Association for the Prevention of Addiction. It was quite influential in affecting social policy about drugs. Rather than everyone trying to brush it under the carpet, bring it out into the open and provide people with the information, particularly parents, so they'll know what's happening if their children go off the rails. They opened various therapy centres around the country. My mother would take me into London sometimes and I would see the addicts injecting heroin in the day centres. I remember walking through Trafalgar Square once and there being a couple of people just slumped down, one of them with an arm hanging with a syringe in it.

I was never into drugs. They were always there, but if you didn't want them, no one forced you into them.

Drugs didn't feature in my life at all. A couple of people I knew smoked cannabis occasionally, but it wasn't my choice. And certainly, I can't remember being aware of people using hard drugs at all. LSD was possibly the biggest thing that was talked about, but I never came across any.

Drugs seemed to die a death in the seventies. There just wasn't that pressure, or expectation, to experiment. Despite all the punk and glam rock, there just didn't seem to be many drugs around. Not for me, anyway.

Wheels

I got my first decent car in the seventies; it was my pride and joy. A Riley in British racing green. The wheels had spats on them. It had a big, long bonnet that lifted up like a gull-wing, and leather seats. I paid £150 for it, which was quite a lot of money then. My dad thought I was mad.

The first boyfriend I ever had, at age fourteen, had a car, and we'd go ice skating together at Queen's in it. But after that, nobody I ever went out with could even drive. I couldn't drive either; I only learnt when I was in my thirties. So the seventies was all buses for me, and walking home late at night, and not really worrying. I always thought, I can run fast, I'll be fine. And I never did have any problems.

We were a non-car generation, and we just got ourselves around on public transport. When I did school sports on Saturday and Sunday mornings I remember standing at bus stops, soaking wet, covered in mud, waiting for buses that never came.

THE FORD CAPRI GXL.
More than ever the car you promised yourself.

At the beginning of the seventies, you were somebody if your family had a car. You were exceptional. By the end of the seventies, all average families had a car, and to be exceptional you had to have a good car, or be a two-car family. My parents had an Austin A40, the original hatchback, bought just after I was born. They had it for thirteen or fourteen years; it rusted away in the end and had to be towed away.

I bought my first car in 1979, a Mark I Escort, the 1966 model. It was a complete rust bucket, the paint was flaking off. I bought a tin of car paint and hand-painted it. Underneath there was a huge hole to bridge, so I used my old Meccano set from when I was twelve – you don't want to spend money on wire gauze, do you? It was a wonderful car.

Orange cars. They invented orange cars then, and the only people who have managed to keep them are the Germans.

My first real boyfriend, in the late seventies, had an orange Vauxhall Viva. He was in the upper sixth and he used to meet me after school in the car. I'd look around and make sure people were looking at me.

I got a Mini when I was seventeen and we'd go off at lunchtime to all the country pubs around Harrogate. Take the school tie off and pretend that the landlord didn't realize we were actually schoolkids.

I had an old Morris Minor, it was quite an icon at my college. We'd get nine or ten of us in there and tool around in it. It finally gave up the ghost when I did the Young's pub crawl in it in 1976, it couldn't pass another MOT.

I had a *DAF* car. They had a lever next to the driving seat, and they only had two gears: one was forwards, and the other was backwards. Dutch. I had a Ford Cortina at one stage; that made me a bit of a laughing stock at university, but at least I was able to keep out of the rain.

I had my mother's car, a Ford Escort estate, which was really good because you could chuck lots of people in the back. It was probably the last decade you could drink and drive and get away with it. And when I think how pissed I was most of the time, it is really,

really scary. I almost mowed down a bus queue one night, about eleven o'clock, because I'd pulled up to talk to this girl – 'ello, darlin', are we goin' to Binge's nightclub? or whatever – and I tried to do the wheel spin as I left, and the wheels were turned the wrong way, and I remember the bus queue scattering all over the place while I tried to get the car back on the road. I got stopped by the police, but they didn't breathalyse me. As long as you could stand up straight, it was, Get along then, son, be careful. Shocking.

We kept making more and more bad cars. My Morris Minor from the sixties was ten times the car the Hillman Avenger was that I bought in the late seventies.

Social change

I used to complain like crazy about having to wear seat belts: I can't drive with this bloody thing on! I can't move! This is a stupid law, absolutely stupid!

I remember walking through a market, and listening to little old ladies who were completely confused by decimalization. I mean, *I* was confused, and I'd had lessons at school about it. And the poor were just gobsmacked by it. Everyone thought they were being ripped off. They probably were.

It was quite sad to see the threepenny bits go. They had a nice feel to them, thick, with those edges. But the pennies were so huge, all that shrapnel in your pocket, holding you down.

In 1971 I used to go to the swimming baths once a week, and at the tuckshop there you could get twelve penny tubes for a shilling. After decimalization I went in with my shilling and asked for the twelve tubes and was told I could only have ten. I was quite put out.

I used to take the Victoria line to school. It was the first new underground line to be built for a hundred years, and it was so modern. Very quiet, very high speed. Because there was nothing that was new in London at the time, nothing. The Victoria line was dragging London into this new century.

I remember getting my first credit card in 1972. I think it was unsolicited, it was simply sent to me by the Midland Bank. And I thought all my Christmases had come at once. I went bananas. Then of course when I got the bill I realized what it was all about, and I cut the card in half. For years afterwards, I got a statement saying they owed me 2p or whatever.

In the seventies my parents moved from an area where they'd grown up, and lived all their lives. All of a sudden, they had the audacity to move to Stalybridge, in those posh sticks. It was a time when people moved further and further away from the community where grandparents lived across the road from you, aunties and uncles lived within walking distance. There was this change

because of cars. It was suddenly quite viable that you move six miles up the road, whereas before you wouldn't have done that. My parents got a bit of stick for it. Oh, they've got ideas above their station, that sort of thing.

Those sixties' tower blocks, all that lunacy. It took them a long time to realize that they were just breeding grounds for muggers and criminals.

One of the big things of growing up in that period in East London was that they had just started to get rid of some of the bombsites from the Second World War. When you think about it, it was nearly thirty years later, and we still had those old prefab houses on bits of waste ground. Enormous swathes of East London were still behind corrugated iron fences, because they were still bombsites from the war, and nobody had built on them. All along the dock area from east of Tower Bridge. It's now all yuppie flats, but then it was bombsites, bombsites, corrugated iron, all over the place.

When I first considered living on my own, in the very late seventies, it was the time of the Yorkshire Ripper. I didn't dare leave home because of that … everyone was very jittery. You thought, it could be anybody. You looked at your neighbours and people on the train and thought, is it him?

When I wanted to apply for jobs, every single phone box within miles had been vandalized.

I've always thought of British society as a series of sheets of glass, where people are stuck inside their sheet of glass, doing the same thing. At the top, the nob's buying a crate of wine, then below that someone's buying a bottle of wine, then below that someone's getting two cans. So you're all essentially involved in the same activity, but you do it within your own sheet of glass. And in the seventies, I felt the only people who could shift between those sheets were gay people or journalists. The one place I met people from outside my own background was the Territorial Army, because the men all came from working-class backgrounds and were escaping whatever: boredom, their jobs, their wives.

I graduated in 1975, got married, bought my first house – for £10,500, a two-bedroom house near Croydon. I didn't actually have a job at the time. I can remember vividly going to the Woolwich Building Society and them saying, How much do you earn? I'd calculated that we had £500 saved from my working on a building site during the summer and what Anne, my wife, had saved; I knew I needed £10,000, and that they'd give you three times your salary. So I thought, if I tell them I earn £3,500 per year, that would be about right. So I told them that, and I didn't even have a job! I got my first mortgage by subterfuge.

Do you remember those computer-type video screens that appeared in pubs? You could play a tennis game on them, called Pong. Looking back, they were incredibly slow and the game was pretty boring, but we thought they were great. They were the forerunners of all the computer games people waste their lives playing today.

Sport

I remember England being knocked out of the World Cup in 1970. Back to normal, after the aberration of 1966. But we'd done it: we'd won it once, no need to do it again. Probably never will.

In 1970, Peter Bonnetti should have been hung, drawn and quartered, the way he played against Germany. Sir Alf Ramsay wanted shooting for taking off Bobby Charlton when we were winning 2-0 because he needed to 'save' the legs of a 31-year-old and brought on Colin Bell.

All those Ali fights – Rumble in the Jungle, Thriller in Manila – were fantastic. Plenty of hype, but great fights. These guys were so heroic. All on the good old BBC.

James Hunt was the greatest thing since Stirling Moss. Long blonde hair, trendy, beautiful birds, yachts, he had it all! Plus he was a great racer and the world champion.

Soccer hooliganism seemed to take off in the seventies. We'd go as a family in the sixties to watch Arsenal play, my mother and sister came with me and my father. Then people started throwing darts at players, and there'd be punch-ups at the grounds. And when the obscene chanting began my father wouldn't let my mother or sister go, then in the end *he* stopped going.

I used to go to Old Trafford with friends, and it was always a slightly iffy situation. I remember travelling from Oxford Road station, and they actually put us in cattle trucks. There was always that frisson of violence in the air.

I went to see a few international cricket matches, and I went to see Desmond Douglas play table tennis, but football more than anything else dominated my life. I went all over following Manchester United. All over, on the Football Specials. If you want to know

about inhuman conditions … it was like going to Auschwitz, it was dreadful, there were no toilets working, that sort of thing. We were treated like scum – so that's how we behaved.

I had a lot of friends who were mad Chelsea supporters, they all lived in Westminster or Fulham. That was the time when football violence was at its peak. Hordes of guys, aged about sixteen to twenty-five, every Saturday would go out and get blitzed drunk, then cause a riot. That was their Saturday afternoon's entertainment.

The disastrous Munich Olympics of 1972 was the first Olympics when sport and politics mixed, and it continued to mix throughout the decade.

I loved tennis, and in the early seventies Dan Maskell was the commentator. It was one of the championships when Martina and Billie-Jean were going great guns. The idea that they were lesbian was becoming pretty current, but not really spoken of. Billie-Jean got knocked out, then Chris Evert beat Martina in a semi-final, so the final was between Yvonne Goolagong and Chris Evert. And when they walked out on court, Dan Maskell almost wet himself, because he was so thrilled to be able to say, And out they come on to the court, these two lovely married girls – and the subtext was, Thank God they've beaten those dykes!

It was probably the decade of England's decline in almost every sport. No, actually, we were pretty good at cricket in the seventies.

I played squash in the seventies. It was a new sport that was starting to boom. I'd never heard of it before I got to university.

Kevin Keegan was the David Beckham of the seventies. Brought to Liverpool from Yorkshire by Bill Shankly, he was an overnight sensation after his debut for the 'Pool. He had this fantastic understanding with John Toshack and they would do these amazing, almost telepathic, one-twos around the box that would produce goal after goal. After winning the European Cup with Liverpool he left them to play in Germany with FC Hamburg. We thought it was the end of football as we knew it, but the next week Bob Paisley went out and bought Kenny Dalglish from Celtic and we forgot all about him. Nice perm though.

The Wider World

A decade of decline, disillusionment – and defiance

Most of Britain's young people were highly politicized in the seventies by dint of the industrial and racial turmoil, not to mention the international epidemic of terrorism, that marked and marred the decade. It started with the three-day week and spiralled downwards into race riots and the Winter of Discontent. But one area of activism gave cause for defiant optimism and confidence: for the vast majority of the girls and women of Britain, the rise of what was then termed 'women's liberation' was the saving grace of the seventies. Lives were changed fundamentally, nothing for women would ever be the same again, and to that most of us say a heartfelt 'Amen!'

Politics: 'Crisis? What crisis?'

The 1970 general election has dramatically affected the rest of my life. Labour were expected to win. There was an amazing quote from Harold Wilson when he saw the first result: 'I don't like the look of that swing.' And of course they lost, and in consequence of that election result we had an era of public spending cuts rather than public spending expansion, and out of that, the long years of university expansion came to a halt. And the whole of my future disappeared. So, instead of working 12–14 hours a day on my research, as I did, thinking it would lead to something else, I was working 12–14 hours a day on my research knowing it would lead to bugger all. I was working my socks off, and what next? Nothing, there was nothing next.

I remember that winter of the three-day week so clearly, sitting in the dark at home. Couldn't watch television. We lived in a very large old house, so it was absolutely freezing cold. Playing cards by the light of a paraffin lamp. Then as the decade unfolded the British economy started to fall to pieces; the manufacturing giant of the world was disintegrating in front of us.

The battle of the three-day week – that was a really seminal winter. There were no streetlights at all, so it was very dark. And sometimes you had heating and light, and then you didn't, and of course it was timed for winter. It was quite extraordinary. If you had electric heating, you were completely stuffed. People went to bed at five or six o'clock, to keep warm.

I blamed the unions. The miners were on strike, there was rubbish piling up in the streets. You'd think, coming from a working-class family, I'd be all for the workers, but I wasn't at all. It was awful.

I had to cook the dinner, because I got home first, before the electricity went off for the evening. It was grim. It was cold, and dark, and all you could do was go to bed and read. You had to get your homework done before the electricity went off. I was cleaning out my mum's kitchen in Devon recently, and she still had all these candles left over from those days. Most of them are bent and warped and covered in dust, you couldn't burn them even if you tried, but she'd never got rid of them.

I remember when the strikes started and we had the candles when it was dark; that was quite exciting for a young teenager. You don't understand the consequences, and it doesn't happen often enough to affect your life, so it was just exciting – and you might have a day off school tomorrow.

The biggest things in the seventies were political things, like the three-day week and the women's movement with those bloody great marches. It became a joke: if you wanted to see your friends, you just went to one of those marches on Saturday afternoons. Everyone was so busy being political.

I was heavily involved in politics on the home front. I'd just got into the world of work as an apprentice, and the three-day week comes along. It was really bad. You had to work maybe a Saturday and a Sunday and a Monday. Well, that really messed me up. Couldn't go to the rugby, or Sunday morning football or whatever.

I grew up in Staffordshire, which is a mixture of very heavy industry, mining and agriculture. The industrial side of things was falling to bits. The miners were on strike, and

BLAKE MORRISON
Born in Yorkshire, he is a poet, a former literary editor, and author of works in every genre, including award-winning memoir *When Did You Last See Your Father?* and an exploration of the Bulger trial, *As If*.

I think the 1970s began around 1973, with power cuts, the oil crisis and the three-day week. Till then, we'd still been living out the 60s – especially those of us who'd been too young to get the most out of them. Sandwiched as they are between a glamorous decade and a clamorous one, the 70s can't help but seem rather drab and low-volume. If their chief attributes had names like the Seven Dwarfs, they'd be called Grungy, Dingy, Mingy, Whingy, Scary, Shadowy and Negative.

I have suppressed all but a few stray memories, but common to all of these is bad taste, including my own. To get married in 1976 I wore a cream suit with flares and platform shoes.

We learned about inflation, and, with the rise of terrorism, we learned about fear. As a student in London, I remember walking nervously past pillar-boxes after the IRA began to leave bombs in them. A different kind of terror gripped the North of England: the serial murders of the Yorkshire Ripper.

To me, the 70s are associated with growing up, and the end of happy illusions. The one good bit was the long hot summer of 1976.

the parents of most of the people I went to school with worked in the potteries, and the potteries were starting to close down.

I was a member of the Young Conservatives when I was at Tech, which I can't believe now. I think it was because I was so disappointed by Labour, with all the strikes. They really seemed to be so dinosaurish and bad for Britain, so I became a Young Conservative.

I became so angry at the way the rich were getting richer, the poor were getting poorer, and nobody gave a flying fuck. I remember wishing that the Baader-Meinhof gang would start up in England, because I would join. We had the Angry Brigade, but it didn't do very much. It was pretty pathetic.

I remember when getting your bags checked going into stores began, but it didn't seem to stop the bombing, did it? We used to go to a curry house in Guildford, and then on to the pubs, so I remember the IRA bombing there in 1974. A bit close to the bone.

We'd gone to Germany for Christmas in 1975 and had a wonderful time, but it was so terrifying coming back through Birmingham because of the IRA bombings. There was about two miles of tunnels to get to the station, and there was this feeling that at any moment there'd be a concrete block coming out of the sky, out of control.

Coming from a rural area we felt quite safe, unaffected by terrorism around the world. We watched it on our TV screens aghast, what was going on in Northern Ireland and London. It seemed very distant.

The Irish troubles were consistently there, but in our house it was always dismissed as the Irish are all mad, so what can you expect?

British politics sucked in the seventies. Everything that led to Thatcherism was happening then. Take the TUC – I mean, talk about selling out the workers. What a mob they were. They wanted their snouts in the trough just as much as the employers did. So you had things like the TUC not being able to work out that things were changing, and they and the workers had to change too. By the time they woke up it was too late. The manufacturing base had all gone, left and gone to Japan, and the workers were left on the scrapheap. They'd been bypassed by the TUC, a mob of dumb bloody Stalinists. Total dinosaurs.

I remember being at a 'new technology' meeting in about 1978, called by the print unions in a hall in Fleet Street. And all these hoary old blokes from the print unions were standing up and saying Well, we'll fight them, and our members won't be doing this, and they won't be doing that. I was there with a colleague, and we stood up and said, Look, you can't ignore this. We need to make agreements, because otherwise we're going to be made irrelevant. And they threw us out. These two bloody great blokes came down the aisle and took us by the elbows and threw us out.

Red Robbo was the shop steward at British Leyland, and he single-handedly destroyed the British car industry.

Nothing worked. You had to wait weeks and weeks to get a telephone line, things like that.

It was so bloody cold. And there were these piles and piles and piles of black garbage bags on every street corner, which got bigger and bigger and bigger, and as the weeks went by, everything in them – even though it was so cold – began to putrefy, they became glurpier and glurpier. Dogs and rats started getting into them. It was really quite disgusting. And it snowed that winter, which isn't very common in London, so you had this slush. And the pavements and the roads were breaking up, because there was no work being done. So you had darkness, garbage and cracked roads.

I remember walking into Leicester Square, and it was filled with oozing black garbage bags and rats running around everywhere. It was like the last days of Pompeii.

The first election I was eligible to vote in was 1979, and I find it impossible to believe that anyone could have voted Labour at the time when all this stuff was going on. Until then I hadn't been interested in politics, but I do remember that at the time, the left wing in Oxford did not mean democratic socialism or egalitarianism.

We didn't believe in politics *per se*. We thought politicians were a bunch of useless idiots in suits and they didn't express our opinions, any of our interests at all – much as the young probably think today. So in the early seventies I believed that it didn't make any difference what you did politically. But by the end of the seventies I had changed my mind about all of that. Probably, feminism was a politicizing thing, and I realized I had more power than I thought I had.

Politics never entered my head. There I was at school learning French, German, English and Latin, but I completely missed the Vietnam War. I didn't know it was on, frankly. I can only recall hearing about them pulling out, and thinking, pulling out of where?

The Emergency — an official announcement

THE 3 DAY WEEK — What it means

From today, everyone in Britain will only be working for three days a week (with the exception of certain exempt classes of person listed below).

EXEMPT PERSONS
Unemployed
Old Age Pensioners
E. Heath Esq.
Night Shift Workers
Vicars
All workers whose work is essential to the country's survival, or who are on strike
Holidaymakers
Aliens under the Offensive Foreign Persons Act 1968
Criminals
Infants below the age of 2-years
Persons deceased since the Emergency Measures came into force
    Following 1 January 1974 it will be illegal for any non-exempt person to work more than three days in any calendar week.
    Fines of up to £3,000 will be imposed upon all those who are found infringing this order.

    Remember—the survival of your country depends upon everyone pulling together and not working for longer than three days.

WILL I GET PAID?
Patrick Moore writes: Well, there are still an awful lot of things we scientists don't know the answer to. But rest assured, in the end there's an answer to everything. And over the next few months, teams of scientists will be working round-the-clock three days a week to come up with an answer to this one. Good night.

WILL BERNARD LEVIN GET PAID?
W.R-M writes: To all who knew him, Bernard Levin came as a great shock.

WILL MILLIONS BE UNEMPLOYED?
    Yes, but only for two days a week. Meanwhile, the country will save millions of pounds a day in wages. So in fact we'll all be better off!

WHAT SHALL I DO WITH THE TIME SAVED?
1. Keep a careful record of all the hours you are not at work. This will give you something to do, and will be very helpful to the Government.
2. If you stay at home, remember that you are not on holiday. Under Article 79 of the Government Panic Measures Act 1973, your home while you are there during normal working hours will constitute a 'workplace'. Therefore the emergency regulations regarding use of fuel, light, heat, TV, etc. must be strictly observed.
    SIT QUIETLY AND TAKE AS LITTLE EXERCISE AS POSSIBLE. This will help to save valuable food-stocks which cannot be distributed owing to the three-day week.

HOW CAN I HELP?
    Thousands of men and women are urgently wanted by the Government to act as 'Work Wardens'. Their job will be to keep a 24-hour watch for all cases of failure to comply with the Emergency Idiotic Measures 1973, and to institute summary on-the-spot fines of up to £200 million on any idle layabout who is found working.

DETECTOR VANS
    During the next few weeks, Government 'work detector' vans will be touring your area, to ensure maximum public co-operation with the new emergency measures. Equipped with highly sophisticated electronic surveillance devices, they are able to 'pick up' heat-traces from anyone engaged in work to a distance of two miles.

This Announcement Is Issued By The Department For Non-Trade and Industry.

It was a time of lots and lots of strikes, when the unions became almost as bad as the management. The management would always try to screw over the unions, but the unions were getting so powerful they were prepared to bring the country to its knees. That whole decade was what brought Maggie into power. Because even working-class people were going, Oh Christ, we've had enough of this.

Everything seemed to be a battle with the unions. I lived in a very Conservative household; both my parents were Tory and they thought England was going to the dogs. But I was a teenager, and nothing was as important to me as what I was doing that weekend, and who I was going out with, that kind of thing.

We were always involved in political discussions, and I was always vaguely left-wing, I dallied with Marxism as many students do. Didn't do that much, I hold my hands up, but I was aware of what was happening in the outside world. The National Front was a big issue. It was a nasty time for some people.

My relatives were very right-wing, although they were working class. They also had a very disconcerting edge of racism to them. They always voted Conservative, and they still do. I voted Labour when I was old enough, as the least worst option at the time.

My parents never ever spoke to me about politics. So when I went to university, I remember sitting there agog as Lesley Newton, who is now a QC, and who I thought came from a similar background to me, talked away in Employment Law class about the TUC, and the Trade Union/Labour Relations Act of 1974.

I think in the seventies, in that fourteen to twenty-four age group, we thought a lot, talked a lot, and did very little. And then, in the following ten years, we started to do something about it.

I've come full circle, because in those days I was very socialist, very left-wing, very radical, and I supported all the strike action. Today I'd be very frightened about the impact on individuals who are trying hard and working hard and doing their best. You look back on your formative years and you think, I must have been so naïve.

I don't think that as a young teenage woman I had any notion of the loss of esteem and power that Britain was experiencing, any sense of humiliation.

All the car workers in Birmingham, masses of them, would meet on this huge hillside and vote publicly. The people who were speaking at these meetings, the shop stewards, were real anarchists. The listeners were sheep. They didn't ask questions. People got what they deserved, I think. In the short term you were coming away with more money, after these massive rises, but everything was doubling in price and it was a spiral. It was madness, really.

We still had a strong industrial base. We still had coalmines, we still had steelworks, we still had a car industry. But the inefficiencies were terrible. Every industry, whether privatized or not, was inefficient. Where I worked, it was still in the forties, nothing had changed from post-war times.

No politicians seem to have been held to account, no one seemed to be holding Heath or Wilson to account for what they were doing. Politicians weren't interrogated. When you listened to the radio in the morning, you had silly old duffers like Jack de Manio on the *Today* programme.

I was a union activist, I believed very strongly in supporting one another, but most of the union activity in the late seventies especially was mindless self-interest. And not to bury bodies during the Winter of Discontent was absolutely diabolical. Labour deserved all they got. They lost, and they should have lost.

JOHN DIAMOND

A columnist on *The Times* who, when stricken with terminal cancer, wrote bravely and hilariously about the progress of his illness in his weekly column. The columns became a play by Victoria Coren and, after his death in 2001, a television film.

1972. A party meeting in the office behind the shop-front which housed the Walthamstow East branch of the Labour Party. Before the estate agents villagized the borough during the 80s property boom, Walthamstow was still a down-at-heel East End suburb and so it was the standard 70s suburban Labour Party crowd of workers by brain rather than by hand which met that evening: some teachers, a few students, council office workers, junior solicitors, and somewhere at the back a couple of quiet blokes who actually laboured manually for a living. We were talking about the miners who were, at that time, on strike. We agreed *nem con* that the strike was essential, that mining was, intrinsically, A Good Thing and coal bosses, even nationalized coal bosses, bad things. But somehow passing a vote of fraternal solidarity didn't feel like genuine political activity, what with the revolution about to start and all, and so after a couple of pints in the Lord Palmerston, some of us drifted over to the rival IS meeting.

The International Socialists was the Trotskyist party of choice that year and in 1972 there was a choice of half a dozen different Trot factions plus sundry Marxist, Marxist-Leninist, Stalinist and Maoist alternatives – because its members actually did things. The things the International Socialists did didn't bring about socialism, of course, or any sort of internationalism, but the IS was very good at demo-arranging, slogan-shouting, hijacking other, more timid organizations and all the other activities tyro politicians were free to pursue if they didn't much have to worry about getting elected.

At the hired schoolroom that was the IS hall we listened to a man (who, as I think back on it now, was probably not long out of his teens) quote some impressive, if random, figures on coal production and then ask us what nights we would be available for picket duty. It hadn't occurred to most of us that students would be allowed to picket anything but their own colleges, and the idea of being allowed to join in real industrial activity was compelling. There were no mines to picket in Walthamstow, of course, but there was a power station up the road in Hackney and a couple of nights later I found myself standing in the drizzle at its gates with a college friend, Siobhan, and half a dozen teenage miners who'd come up from Kent. We don't think of well-set Sandwich and its environs as a mining town these days, but thirty-odd years ago (and indeed until 1989) the Betteshanger colliery was still bringing up Kentish coal, and here we were standing, fuzzy pink cheek by rough sooty jowl, with real miners.

The Betteshanger lads were bemused by our idolatry: they came from a village where fifteen-year-old school leavers could choose only between tedious and badly paid work in the local shoe factory and tedious, back-breaking but slightly better paid work in the mines. Given any sort of real choice they'd have avoided either and they couldn't quite understand why we, their contemporaries, who were being paid a public subsidy for going into a warm college every day, would want to spend cold evenings round a bonfire asking dumb questions about the dignity of labour.

One of the lads shuffled over to me. Is she your bit of skirt then? Siobhan snorted a laugh: it would be a couple of years before word would filter down to eighteen-year-old girls that such questions should be considered inappropriate, as, indeed, should be the appellation 'girls'. The miner found this even more confusing: what sort of partnership could there be between an eighteen year old boy and girl other than a sexual one?

It was a successful night for the strike: not a single coal lorry got through the gates of the power station. Then again, though, it was a pretty lousy night for me, Siobhan and the teenage miners: not a single lorry tried.

It was only the Winter of Discontent that was shambolic, it wasn't a decade of shambles at all. The number of working days lost in strikes in the seventies was very, very low compared with European averages. Suddenly this devastating, huge inflation swept across Europe. I mean, we'd never had anything like that in our history before, it was like Germany in 1922. And it just washed people away. But the union reaction was absolutely pathetic, and what happened was pathetic.

The arrogance of a teenager meant that I was totally unaware of Britain's decline in the seventies. You live in your own head, and you're more interested in what happens to you than what happens around you. I never even watched the news.

I remember the Green Goddesses of 1978–79, and how frightening it all was, when you thought about it deeply. It made me more politically aware, although I wasn't conscious of it at the time.

Anarchy was intellectually acceptable; lots of people belonged to the Socialist Workers' Party, the Communists. Even at that time, the National Union of Students was considered a left-wing organization of people like Jack Straw, who was perceived as a dangerous left-winger.

I wasn't a right-winger politically, in the sense of having a thought-out Conservative scheme, nor was I a wet Liberal by inclination. But there I was, in the volunteer reserve. I certainly remember conversations in the seventies about subversion in which one had the feeling one was being sounded out – it could always be laughed off afterwards as late-night talk – as to whether in the event of the Wilson government doing something perceived to be injurious to the nation's or the Queen's interest, whether there wouldn't come a time when we'd have to be called upon to take action. I'm sure people would deny it now, but I'm pretty certain that at the time there was an undercurrent of sounding people out as to whether there could be a military coup.

We forget the Cold War now, but I spent the best part of ten years thinking that the enemy was the faceless hordes that would come streaming across. It was very, very real in a way that now seems laughable.

I was not a very aware beast, politically or even socially. My father had been a miner, and had moved to steel in South Wales. Then a lot of people were laid off at the steelworks, and I began to notice the stress that my father was under. But I wasn't writing radical diaries in the evening, I would be thinking much more selfish thoughts like where was my next party going to be?

I didn't have a clue. My father kept saying, Come and watch the news, and I wasn't interested at all. But with interest comes exasperation and disgust, doesn't it?

I didn't know anything about Vietnam, I was a teenager, I wasn't interested. All I cared about was make-up and when I was getting my next pair of jeans, and what I'd be doing on Saturday night, and who was snogging who.

As students in the seventies, we'd lost the innocence of 'we're going to help change the world'. I remember one incident at our college – there was one of these strikes going on and we were close to taking some exams. And the National Union of Students decided that, in solidarity with the rest of the union movement, they were going to call a strike. And the big debate was, Do we as students cross the picket lines to take these exams? Our lecturers made it clear: the exams are going to be there, if you want to take them. If you don't take them, we can't guarantee that you'll be able to resit within the year, or whatever. And I can remember vividly deciding with another two or three students that we were going to take these exams. A lot of students from other parts of the college turned up and tried to stop us. We were shouted at, but they didn't stop us.

I was much more interested in economics than politics, and there was something fundamentally wrong with the economy at that point. Whether it was too many working days lost through strikes, or a complete lack of interest in actually doing any work, or the fact that we were still struggling with an industrial base that didn't make sense any more, we were not competitive in the world, nobody wanted to buy the stuff we kept making. Looking back on it, I can see that all of those things were partly to blame.

The whole of the seventies was riddled with economic mismanagement, unfortunately. That's why everyone voted for Mrs Thatcher.

'Women's lib': the female perspective ...

My awareness of the women's movement started when I got hold of a copy of *The Female Eunuch*. So many people say that that book changed their lives. And it did. I couldn't begin to tell you now what was in it that changed my life, except I know it did. I walked through a door and never went back.

I read *The Female Eunuch*, and that book changed my life. But I have also to say that recently I read a piece by Germaine Greer in which she wrote about her sadness about not having had children, and I thought, Well, thanks, Germaine, because you're the reason I didn't have children either. Because that book made me terrified of the trap of being a wife and a mother, and being dependent on a man for money.

We finally came into contact with the writings of people like Simone de Beauvoir, who was saying 'Liberation starts in the pocket'. It was a new mantra for us to chant. It was great!

I was outside the classic middle-class feminist activist circles, the educational club, so I was very aware of how middle class the women's movement was, and how excluded working-class women felt. I was desperately pressing my nose up against the window of the women's movement, and I didn't find my way into it until quite late on. So I felt great kinship with black women and working-class women, who said, Hey, don't talk for us. The movement became a very exclusive club for about twenty women, who all talked to each other, at one stage.

Once I got into the women's movement, I took off like a rocket. I felt as if I'd really found where I belonged.

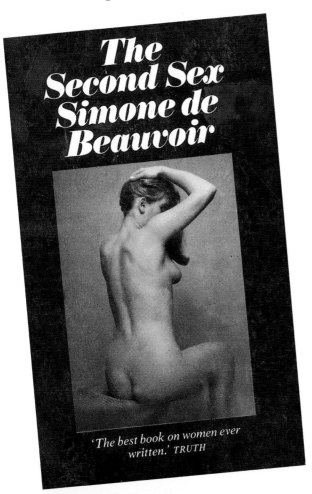

'The best book on women ever written.' *TRUTH*

The expectations of women changed totally in this decade. The be-all and end-all was not to be someone's secretary. It was a very short time for this change to come about, and I think the impetus for that came from England.

Our mothers' generation was totally stymied. My mother should have been the chairman of a large corporation, but of course it was utterly impossible for her. Women of my generation had no such constraints, and that was thanks to the women's movement of the seventies. It changed everything. Women were doing it for themselves in a way that hadn't happened since Mrs Pankhurst kicked the bucket.

In 1977 my three-year relationship with my boyfriend broke up. I was really upset about it, I was still in love with him but there was something wrong, I knew I had to leave the relationship although I didn't know why. Then I discovered feminism, and realized what had been wrong. He was a complete control freak. He wouldn't even let me drive. I had tried for three years to be something I wasn't.

I had a circle of great girlfriends. We were all reading Virago books left, right and centre, and we all started to think in feminist terms. It was really exciting. We realized you don't have to live under this regime of men, you don't have to be what they want you to be, you can just be yourself and have fun.

I never assumed I'd be anything other than a managing director. It was a wonderful time to grow up, for a female, because the world was there: go and get it. It was never assumed by my parents that I would just get married and have children.

My dad's big ambition for me was to be an air hostess: a nice career for girls. And that was so not what I was into. I was into women's lib; it dawned on me that I could have a career, live independently.

JOYCE HOPKIRK

Now a novelist. Edited several women's pages in Fleet Street before being appointed first editor of the British *Cosmopolitan*, launched in 1972 with a scoop centrefold of Germaine Greer's husband and a scoop story on Michael Parkinson's vasectomy.

As an ex-prefab dweller (tin bath in front of the fire), failed 11-plus entrant and with no university degree, I remember the 1970s as a can-do society. When I helped launch the British edition of *Cosmo* in 1972, the passport to success and prosperity lay more in the belief in your own abilities rather than qualifications. Thank God for that. Today you can hardly get a job as a taxi-driver without a degree.

Cosmo hit the stands and sold out in 24 hours because it was miles away editorially from the rather starchy feminist tomes around then – *Spare Rib, Nova* and the publisher Virago. Helen Gurley Brown, founder of the American magazine and originator of the concept of 'the Cosmo girl', had received worldwide notoriety for her book *Sex and the Single Girl*, in which she claimed any woman could get any man if she followed her advice and played the right cards. Although the British edition didn't have such a desperate air about it – catching a man wasn't statistically the difficult job it appeared to be in New York – we still captured the public imagination, helped by a nearly-nude, male pin-up in the centrefold. The idea that women might make the running in the sex game was intriguing to both sides and although we British journos preached that women wouldn't be valued if they lived their lives entirely through men, we did acknowledge that it was much more fun to have one at your side. This uncoquettish approach appealed to women in the 70s. We had enjoyed for nearly a decade freedom from unwanted pregnancies thanks to the Pill, and were beginning to be paid the rate for the job, regardless of gender. Once the critics could see that *Cosmo* was more than just a sex guide and provided a real service in the way of career and relationship advice they backed off, and even wrote for our pages. It was a great time to be female if you had self-belief – and, boy, did we work hard to get that message across.

I was not arsey at all about feminism. I would have loved to have been Farrah Fawcett-Majors, or any Charlie's Angel really.

I hadn't come from a strong family of women in terms of role models, and certainly at school the message hadn't come through in the early days of my high school, but once I hit the sixth form I was taught by women who hadn't needed to marry, who were earning a good income and were getting along on their own, and who had opinions. And I could see, certainly, a woman like my English teacher not being browbeaten by men but holding her own. It was highly impressive.

When I got to college, I was mixing with women who had chosen a career over a family. That was a real eye-opener for me, the possibility of making your own way. And I realized that access to money wasn't denied to me the way it had been to my mother. She couldn't buy that miraculous twin-tub that she slaved over on HP without my father's consent. I could negotiate my own bank loan. So I was the first female member of my family to have control over her own money, to have her own bank account.

... and the male perspective

My sister, who is eight years older than I am, embraced the traditional woman's role – big white wedding, stay at home, all that stuff. I was fairly broadminded, and feminism seemed to me to be a reasonable thing. The anti-feminism thing made me angry, I couldn't see the point.

I was a male chauvinist pig until I got married, when I was shown the error of my ways. My mother did everything, all the housework, cleaning, washing up, everything. She'd do me a separate dinner from my father, because we ate at different times. She'd even cook up two different lots of baked beans, because we liked different brands.

I went to a boys' school, and I didn't have a sister so I had absolutely no idea. My ideas came from the James Bond films: women as disposable consumables. And perhaps girls sensed that. I might as well have had a sign above my head saying, Run a mile, *now*.

I found the women's movement worrying and troublesome, it was so militant: all men were complete shits. Not that a swing in that direction wasn't in some ways justified.

I always thought women were wonderful creatures and we should be on an equal par with them. It certainly worried me when they began to feel they were superior to men in virtually every respect. That made me quite scared of women, quite scared, for some time.

The environment movement

I remember February 1970 as being incredibly, unseasonably warm. We wore T-shirts and sat outside drinking in pub gardens. That seemed to be the start of 'global warming'.

I can remember sitting in a lecture in 1975 when I was about sixteen. I was doing a subject called Environmental Studies, which was a new subject, and being told about the Greenhouse Effect.

I worked as a volunteer for Friends of the Earth when Jonathon Porritt was the director, in a tiny little office tucked into Islington. He was very sophisticated, the first person I heard talking about using the UN as a forum for environmental change. I thought, Wow, this is really big. But I got really sick of licking envelopes.

Even in the seventies, I knew that the world's agriculture was based on a finite resource. We weren't into organic farming, we were into using the phosphate resource. My influences came from geography teachers. The question was, how do you feed a population of three and a half billion without using phosphates? And the answer is, you don't; basically, you starve.

At university, you didn't worry about the environment. You bought the cheapest food you could, so that you'd have money left over for beer. There was a sop to the environment, but that's all.

It was my generation that made the environment an issue. I was very into it in the eighties, but in the seventies … I did have a Save the World T-shirt.

I remember being given the message about never wasting paper in the early seventies, and it really struck a chord with me and I never ever forgot it. People hadn't been aware of it at all before then. I was never passionate enough to join anything, but I was always careful not to waste anything, to turn lights off, that kind of thing. The message got through.

1977 VOLE 1 60p

Vole

Fleet Street flayed!
Windscale power games
The cost of noise
Killer Jubilee trees!
What IS going on in Herefordshire?
John Arlott sings!
Concrete teeth

Preservation of the countryside was important to me. House building on the greenfield sites, although we didn't call them that then, was an issue then. We didn't recycle then, or worry much about fuel, but in our wishy-washy liberal way we knew that resources were finite and we had to take care.

In the seventies I felt strongly that we needed a more communal sort of lifestyle, and a more ecologically sensitive sort of lifestyle. I have always hated whatever government is in power, and it's never been possible to like any of them on environmental grounds.

You didn't worry about the environment, you didn't worry about pollution. Nobody worried about anything, it was quite hedonistic.

The *Amoco Cadiz* disaster happened in March 1978. I remember going to a party round about then and just getting lambasted about being a filthy bastard working in the oil business, how we were going to destroy the world and all the rest of it. But the *Amoco Cadiz* was a real milestone. There was a growing awareness that there was a problem, and it was the start of big legislative changes over safety and the environment.

I remember when London was really dirty. It didn't have the same attitude to litter or refuse. It wasn't culturally unacceptable to just dump stuff then.

There was a hell of a lot less traffic in the seventies. But we still used leaded petrol, so there was that smell in the air you don't get any more.

I remember the conversion to natural gas. I was living at home, and the front path was dug up to lay new gas pipes. That was definitely part of a movement towards a cleaner world.

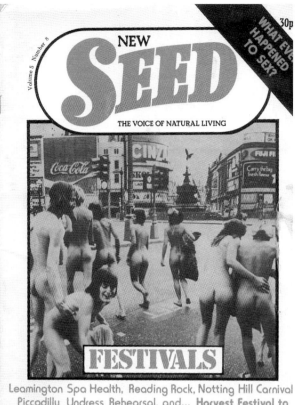

Volume 5 Number 8

30p

WHAT EVER HAPPENED TO SEX?

NEW **SEED**

THE VOICE OF NATURAL LIVING

FESTIVALS

Leamington Spa Health, Reading Rock, Notting Hill Carnival Piccadilly Undress Rehearsal, <u>and</u>... Harvest Festival to Hallowe'en~ The 'Moody' Season? PLUS ∙ PUMPKINS ∙ PICKLES ∙ HERBAL SKIN CARE ∙ NATURAL FARMING

The Thames got a lot cleaner in the seventies. Fish came back.

Race relations

My friend and I were involved in the Rock Against Racism movement. Mainly because there was always a really good concert at the end, such as Elvis Costello and The Clash, but also because skinheads were then rising up and we really hated them and their racism. So we went on the marches and to the concerts, and wore the badges, thousands of us. It was really exciting.

I really got into Rock Against Racism. The rise of the National Front had become quite apparent, and young people finally got off their bums and began to do something about it.

The Bengali community became established in the East End in the seventies, and people like

CAITLIN MORAN

Now the pop and TV critic for *The Times*. The eldest of eight children of a rock musician, brought up in a Wolverhampton council house, and educated at home by her former flower-child mother. At twelve she won a children's writing contest; at seventeen she published her first novel, *The Chronicles of Narmo*.

My first recollection is of frustration with the fact that Penelope Pitstop was the most beautiful woman in the world, but the strictures of competing in the Wacky races and being pursued by the Hooded Claw meant that she always dressed in trousers and crash helmet, and not the sticky-out dress with pink sash that such a princessy lady should obviously be wearing.

The 1970s were the last decade before wall-to-wall carpeting became mandatory, and I remember spilling orange squash on the non-carpeted bit of floor that remained sticky for what seemed three or four years. I would press my foot on to the stickiness and lift it off again, because it felt nice.

The council came round and replaced all our roofs because of the asbestos scare and the garden turned yellow with dust and when we came in Mum had to brush us down with a hairbrush. We had Space Hoppers, which we called Bounce Hoppers, and used as weapons. It was mandatory to wear dungarees, and I was so confused by all the straps and buttons and clips I wet myself before I got them off. All the kids in Wolverhampton wore wellies and, when they came in, moon-boots. There were no trainers, and every kid had a red plimsoll line halfway up their calves where the tops of the wellies rubbed.

I remember Dad explaining that Ian Dury's 'Hit Me With Your Rhythm Stick' wasn't actually a cue to start hitting the littlest kid with our plastic golf clubs, and that the rhythm stick was a drumstick. So we stole Dad's drumsticks and hit the kid with them instead. We went sledging down the stairs on a tray because we'd seen it on *The Banana Splits*, and broke the legs of Mum's bureau. I dressed a life-sized baby doll in our youngest sibling's clothes and dropped it out of the bedroom window so it passed the living room window and scared our parents to death.

As far as we were aware, there weren't any strikes and there wasn't a government. The world outside was something that would happen in the future. The 70s for me meant lots of hitting my brothers and sisters. We hadn't discovered sarcasm then – that only kicked in around the time of Spandau Ballet.

me and my friends would head off to Brick Lane to eat great, cheap food. Then the people around Whitechapel became the targets of the National Front: shit and petrol put through letterboxes and so on, skinhead attacks on young people. It meant more to us because we actually went and ate there, met the people.

Remember the oil crisis? The OPEC countries got together and decided to raise the price of oil. And that made everyone in England very anti-Arab. It had a huge effect, because it was followed shortly afterwards by all these Arabs coming to live in London. And they were the only people who had any money, and everyone thought, that's *our* money. I've never seen such racism or incipient racism happen almost overnight.

The National Front was alive and well in Britain in the seventies, and we were very, very anti-them. I went to one riot in Lewisham in the late seventies that was extremely violent, and it was a real shock. The National Front were going to march through an area of Lewisham that was very black, just to show their strength. SDP was a student organization on the extreme left, and it too was violent. We were all milling around together, expecting the National Front to come, and I remember seeing them coming around the corner. They had these huge flags, but more scary than that, they had an enormous number of very big horses on either side of them. This was the police, who were accompanying them. It was like the Russian Revolution. At this point, everyone went into a panic, and somebody grabbed hold of my hands and pulled me, and before I knew it I was in the front line to stop these people and horses. I managed to split away from that just in time but I got squashed up against an empty shop window (this was a typical seventies street scene: empty houses, empty shop windows). The SDP was lined up on the other side, which had houses. They started throwing bricks at the National Front, and a lot of them were misfiring and were going through the shop windows on the side I was on. I was being pressed back against all this cut glass. And I couldn't move. Then the police suddenly cordoned off our one exit, and we couldn't get out. It was really frightening. There was all this orange tear-gas, and afterwards my nose was all orange. I sat on the bus going home thinking, I don't think I'll go to another riot.

We really wanted a world where black and white were integrated, because there were so many black people, especially where I was living in south London, who were making really great contributions in terms of music, for one thing, and just sheer attitude. West Indians would walk down the street like gods, with ghetto blasters on their shoulders. But they were still being oppressed. If you walked down Brixton on a Saturday night there were cops stopping everyone black.

There were only two West Indian girls in my year at school, not even in my class. There was no real integration. I lived in a very white, mainly Jewish area.

Wolverhampton in the seventies was a miserable place really, the inheritance of Enoch Powell. It had a big black population, not so much Asian as West Indian, and there were some serious problems.

I encountered my first person of non-white ethnic origin at something like the age of thirteen, because I came from a rural, northern background. This made me either too PC or too tolerant; when I finally mixed with people from different racial backgrounds, I wanted to be too PC with them.

I never came across any racial tension. I lived in the middle of an Asian community, and I had a great time with them in the seventies. We played in a cricket league that had an Indian team, a Pakistani team, a West Indian team. I couldn't see any problems at all, even though I heard about race riots and all that.

Which was the truer representation of British people's attitude to black people, *Love Thy Neighbour* or Alf Garnett? Were we just paying lip service to the idea of racial equality? I think some people took these programmes too seriously. We all make fun of ourselves, we should be able to laugh together.

Apparently, Asian people were really happy with *It Ain't Half Hot, Mum* because the punkah-wallah in it spoke Hindi and Punjabi and Urdu fluently. But it was also because there was a black man on the telly, not just someone blacked up.

In 1974, for the first time in my life as a Labour supporter, I found myself at a polling station with representatives from the National Front. Normally you just have a very polite conversation with the people from the Liberals or the Conservatives or whatever, but here were these two horrific guys from the National Front, and I just couldn't speak to them. There was no question of talking to them because they were beyond the pale. Something happened up at the council offices in Cheshunt, and a lot of us who were in the Anti-Nazi League went up there to protest about these horrible people from the National

Front. But we were there with banners for the Anti-Nazi League, and the National Front went along with cameras and took pictures of all of us. We thought, Next, they're going to turn up at our houses, aren't they? 'We know where you live.' It was very, very intimidating. You stood there, but there was somebody clicking at every face. And you thought, I don't like this.

I knew that racism was wrong, but I wasn't involved. There weren't many black faces in our school, and I think there was a lot of racism there because of ignorance. I'd have marched, but it never came up.

Some Maltese boys came to the school when I was about fourteen and they were so gorgeous, so exotic. But that was about as close as we got in Ilkley.

I was absolutely unaware of any race problems in the seventies. I had a rural childhood, and the University of East Anglia then had very few black or even non-British students. Those there were terribly popular because they were seen as exotic. I led a very sheltered life!

In the seventies, there were certain parts of south London that you just didn't go into at night if you were white. Then again, there were parts of east London you didn't go into if you were white or black or whatever.

Travel
I got my first girlfriend when I was thirteen, on holiday. She was from Barnes. We went to Barnes and I thought we'd gone to the end of the world.

I used to get a bus ticket called a Red Rover, and I went to Chislehurst in Kent because there are some caves there that were used as bunkers in the Second World War. It really wasn't very far from where I lived but I thought it was like another planet, way out in the countryside. We lived in a tiny little world.

In 1970 a group of friends and I took off around the world in a 1935 Bristol double-decker bus. We'd spent about a year doing it up, then we tried to get sponsorship – with limited success – and off we went. It was a time when you could do that, when borders were still open and you didn't think much about the dangers.

We went on the hippie trail to India and South-East Asia at the end of 1973, in a Kombi. It was amazing. You could go straight through in those days, right across Afghanistan and Iran and Pakistan. My Western ideas of towns copped a bashing when we reached places like Afghanistan, where buildings were made of mud and were full of animals. Rows of mud buildings with murky lamp-lit interiors lining the dirt roads, camel trains swaying down the main streets. It was all so exotic and mysterious and Eastern.

Every boyfriend I'd ever had had gone off on the hippie trail, and I was left behind, so in 1973 I decided to go to India and Afghanistan myself. But I only had forty quid. Two girlfriends and I hitched across Europe. One got as far as Cologne, then came home, but I hitched with Kerry to Amsterdam and across to Turkey. But then I had to admit defeat and ring my dad up, and he sent me the fare home. The Orient Express was £26, back from Istanbul to London.

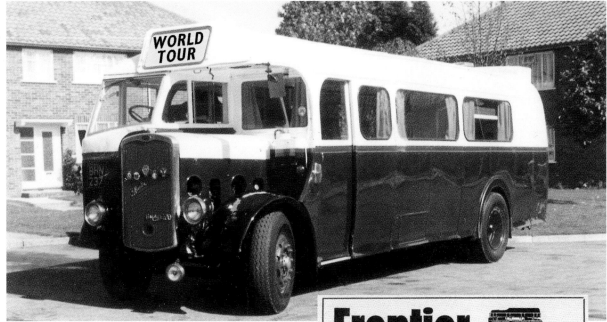

My boyfriend and his friend went overland across Europe and Asia in 1976 on the Magic Bus. The bus couldn't get up the Alps so they had to go around, then they broke down for three weeks in Iran. It was a complete nightmare. Half the windows had gone, so it was freezing cold and you couldn't sleep. They set off with sandwiches, and the journey took an extra six weeks, so all they had were these mouldy sandwiches. They'd arrive in the middle of the night somewhere and they never had the right currency so they couldn't buy food. They spent the whole time pushing the Magic Bus.

I hitched around Europe when I was sixteen, then did it by Inter-rail when I was seventeen. We did loads of hitchhiking, which doesn't happen now.

In the seventies I travelled on my own for the first time, feeling quite safe to hitchhike. I hitchhiked across the nation, across France and over to Poland on my own, and I didn't feel afraid.

In the mid-seventies I went across to the United States on my own. It cost me fifty-nine quid to go to New York with Freddie Laker's airway, and I didn't feel afraid to do it because there were other young women doing it at the time.

Frontier International

Cosmopolitan Girls Go Frontier Style to Frontier Country

Overland and Jet/Overland adventure holidays to Morocco and the Sahara, Russia, Scandinavia and the Arctic Circle, Greece, Turkey, India and Israel

Send for our new 1972 Full Colour Brochure

TINA BROWN
Founder and editor-in-chief of *Talk* magazine in New York. Emerged from Oxford in 1974 to take on Fleet Street, becoming Young Journalist of the Year by 1978, before going on to edit *Tatler* in Britain and *Vanity Fair* and *The New Yorker* in New York.
The 1970s brought the rise of hack-power when *Private Eye* dandruff became a shower of gold and the media was the glamour profession of choice. It was the era of Little Keith, the hero of Martin Amis's *Dead Babies*, and the pissed-off politics of three-day weeks. Good for satire, street-smart writers and angry productions at the Bush Theatre and the King's Head. The *New Statesman* under Anthony Howard was the intellectual HQ of the cool, counter-intuitive crowd – Amis, Hitchens, Barnes, Fenton, Russell Davies. I used to wait outside the newsagent's in the Woodstock Road (when I was at Oxford) on Fridays, to see this week's delicious demolition of some sacred cow's new book. Ian Hamilton's *New Review* was cooler still, the place where Clive James did his best stuff, confident that the circulation was smaller than the masthead. Book reviews were de-constructed in Greek restaurants in Soho, but the beer-mats of the Bush held the suppressed energy of the future. Or so it seemed to me, as I saved up my Catherine Pakenham Award money to run away from the rain and go to America where I planned to wait out the rest of the 70s, a decade of darkest irony and clever journalism.

We first went abroad when I was fifteen, in 1974. It was the first time for all of us. My mother had never been on a plane before either. We went to Spain, to Almuñécar, and we all got a real buzz out of it. It was amazing, it all seemed so glamorous and special.

I went to university and after two years I left and taught English at a school in Toulon, in France, and travelled from there. I learnt to parachute and ski in French, which I thought was a very good way to learn the language, because I had to concentrate so much on what I was doing. I bought a VW van with some others and we would travel down into Spain, or go towards Italy, and we'd run out of money and have to watch people eat sandwiches for a couple of days, and look through litter bins for our main meal.

I was always at least ten years behind the times, emotionally and sexually. In 1978, I went on that round-the-world trip my contemporaries had been on years before. The one where you go to Nepal. But by the time I went, Persia had become Iran, and effectively closed down, and the overland trip was no longer so practical. So I flew to Sri Lanka, into India and up into Nepal.

I kept thinking I saw people from college, with the Afghan coat and the straggly hair, but when I caught up with them I realized it was someone else. All the people in Nepal were completely the same, but they weren't my friends from ten years before – who now, having been hippies, were running accounts for Coca-Cola.

In the summer of 1975 I went down with five friends to Morocco in an old VW van with paintings on the sides. That was a big adventure. Then I backed the van into somebody in the queue for the ferry at Algeciras. That caused a bit of a do, especially as those vans were very poorly viewed by customs officials. We had a lot of stops and searches, but we rather liked the attention.

There was full employment then, so it was not uncommon to take a year off to travel the world before settling down to a job. Whereas my experience when I travelled as a backpacker twenty years later was that people were doing it within university, or had worked for several years and were going back to a job or a house. Quite different from that Dylan-influenced, Kerouac *On the Road* style of people in the seventies.

Moving on: into the eighties

I remember the night that Margaret Thatcher got in. I was at a very grand twenty-first birthday party, sitting next to someone who'd been to Harrow. And he said to me, Isn't it marvellous, the Tories have got in again, and I said I think it's an absolute disaster, and he didn't speak to me again. But I knew at that point that everything was going to change.

At the end of the seventies *Brideshead Revisited* was on television, and that was a defining thing. It was like the start of a new era, because the life we led at St Andrews was exactly like *Brideshead Revisited*, still like seventy years ago in a wonderful way. And that was the beginning of the eighties for me. That brought with it much more of a feeling of entitlement. I went up to university in 1978 with that bleak seventies attitude, but by the time I left I was already a yuppie.

By the end of that decade, the technology had flattened the workers, moved on, and given birth to Mrs Thatcher. I'll never forget that day. I woke up on the Sunday morning after the election when Mrs Thatcher had won, and I thought, I don't want to stay in this country, I'm getting out. It took me a few years but I did.

The whole decade led up to that moment when Thatcher was voted in. It was a period when the economy and society, anything to do with earning a living, was changing, and the TUC either wouldn't get it or couldn't get it. Car factories closed down, things went offshore, shipbuilding, the steel industry – do you remember that Elvis Costello song 'Shipbuilding', which was an absolute lament, a wonderful song. The whole country was being dismantled. And the TUC was still thundering on about We won't accept this, We demand this, We'll stand firm. Just like Canute.

Britain in the late seventies was just ripe for something really revolutionary. And no matter what Thatcher did, people were going to say,

Hey, it's gotta be better than we've got now.

Thatcher's election was the most depressing thing that had happened to any of us. We were just horrified. I think she personified for us everything that was really evil, before she even proved the point. You just knew she was really bad news. But England was going through such a crisis. There were huge unemployment figures, and I think whoever came into power would probably have felt they had to do something. But what she did was basically sacrifice one half of the country in order that the other half should live, which seemed very brutal.

We got back to London from travelling in the Far East in November 1979, and it was grey and cold, and we were wearing flip-flops, and tropical clothes. Thatcher was in, and the joy had gone out of it. The happiness of being back with family lasted about a day.

I hated Thatcher on the one hand, but intellectually she was a warrior. She was a class warrior, she did the business, and she made the others seem wimpy, particularly the Labour politicians.

When Thatcher came in I thought, new broom. I did not know what to expect, but I thought what I had known in my limited life had not worked. So, keep our fingers crossed and let's hope.

To be frank, it could not have got any worse. And I don't care what anybody's politics are; I have never voted Conservative in my life, yet I am a great admirer of Margaret Thatcher. This country was on its knees by the end of the seventies, and the only person who could have changed it was somebody who was extremely tough and extremely arrogant. She was the right person at the right time.

The depressing thing for us was that Thatcher was a woman, and she behaved just like the worst kind of man. The ultimate irony. People kept pointing it out, and you couldn't deny it.

She did a lot for this country. She did a lot of damage, too.

Whoever came in and changed things for the better, there was going to be a lot of trouble, a lot of damage. You can't make an omelette without breaking eggs.

We were declining into an island off the coast of Europe, but that's the reality. That's what we are.

The end of the seventies for me was a frightening time of life. I thought, Shit, I'm going to have to grow up here. I was scared of growing up. I didn't want to get a job, I wanted to stay in education because it was safe. I was frightened of going to work.

I felt worried about things as the decade came to a close, but broadly optimistic. Things would sort themselves out. I was still idealistic. It was only in the eighties I became more cynical.

I was very optimistic, going into the eighties. My life was going to take off.

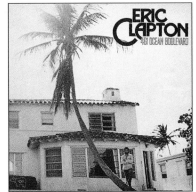